Council of Angels

Jo Long

Mayhaven Publishing

Mayhaven Publishing
P O Box 557
Mahomet, IL 61853
USA

All rights reserved.
No part of this book may be reproduced or transmitted in any form or
by any means without written permission
from the publisher, except for the inclusion
of brief quotations in a review.

Copyright © 1999 Jo Long
Original Drawings Copyright © 1999 Crystal Black
Cover Design by Cullen J. Porter
First Edition—First Printing   1999   1 2 3 4 5 6 7 8 9 10

Library of Congress Number: 99-74545
ISBN: 1-878044-74-5

To Edna —
Pleasures await as each day Breaks
The things of beauty God has for You
Love
Jo Long

P.O. 415
Argenta, Il. 62501

Dedication

To my family and special friends who encouraged me to keep searching through mystery after mystery.

Introduction

Astounding as it might seem, I have two small boys and a very dear friend to thank for my present way of life. The boys for letting me know that I, alone, was not enough to solve their needs; my friend for involving me in her search to understand her conflict. In searching together to find answers, we found much more than we could ever have imagined.

We found strength greater than evil; forces greater than legalities; riches in excess; peace of mind and a new concept of love.

Sharing my personal experiences, as they actually took place, is my way of introducing my way of life to you.

The Bible is full of messages received from God. Jesus' disciples reported these "dreams" and "voices" carefully.

Most modern religious leaders pray to the Father, the Son and the Holy Spirit, but contact from spirits are branded as the deceptive work of the Devil. What a contradiction! How discouraging it must be to pray to the Trinity for years and to receive nothing except from Demons.

True believers still get messages from the Holy Spirit. They still believe there are many, many angels active in this world today. If the messages and the angels are full of love and good works, follow their lead and have faith.

We cannot understand all.

Editor's Note

There will be some who will read this book and think of it as one woman's effort to cope with all things physical and spiritual. Others may see it as a physical and spiritual manifestation in one woman's life. Whatever the perspective of the reader, this small book provides absorbing questions about the limitations and creations of the soul.

First Light

I caught my breath.
My body froze in fright.
My rigid fingers extended to their fullest reach, flinging the pencil free across the room.
The words I was writing had no meaning to me.
I looked at the words. Each one of them. Then at each sentence.
Oh leader of my soul where art thou at a time of reckoning?
Now what the heck did that mean?
Look up and be pleased.
Well, I was more than pleased. I was exhilarated. It was not important that I understood the meaning. I had heard and written down words.
Go do my bidding.
Who's bidding? I wasn't frightened now, just amazed.
I stared at what I had written and the thought flashed through my mind that I should keep a record of the things I heard. The date was May 22, 1974.

I wondered if I could do it again. I started to think "The Lord's Prayer." "Our father who. . ." Immediately the words came again, overriding the prayer.

Let the boys be your's, we will be here with you. It is not as it seems, but beyond your dreams. You will be blessed. It is good. Happiness. So many things to be said. Look in 'Acts 13.'

I did know what this was about. The two little boys the court had awarded us six weeks before. They were brothers. We called them Bear and Chigger.

Chigger, age two, was in diapers and believed he was a one-man demolition team. His energy was boundless and his agility unbelievable. Those chubby little hands went in four directions at one time, and it was plain to see his mind was way ahead of his hands. The short, chubby legs had one speed—fast. His round, cherubic face was quick to light up in a smile. Blue eyes danced with enthusiasm, and his glee made me wonder if there was some enjoyment I was missing.

Bear was three going on forty. He was a head taller than Chigger, thin, quiet and, although upset by the sudden turn his life had taken, was more concerned about Chigger than himself. He had dark brown hair over his serious blue eyes and a soft voice. He was slow moving and content to quietly sit and observe his new surroundings. Often he would gently correct Chigger by steering him away from some probable catastrophe. People often ignored Bear due to the constant attention Chigger demanded.

I looked in "Acts 13" and read the first verse. It told me

nothing. I was so excited about finally writing and about receiving the words, that I didn't wonder about the meaning of the verse. Besides, I had no more time to wonder. My family was coming home.

I greeted my husband as he walked through the door.

"Guess what. I can write!"

Art's answer was, "Oh yeah? Guess what. So can I."

I held my notebook up to Art's face, "See, this is my first real writing!"

My husband carefully looked at it and frowned, studying the many letters and few words. "How do you account for this?"

"I can't. Sybil was here and we talked about all of her writings, and before she left I knew I could write. I don't understand it, but neither does Sybil. She gets the writing, usually doesn't know what it's about, and then after a while something will happen and she will know what to do about it. Sorta' like she's been prepared for something before it has even happened."

His only comment was, "Hummmmm," with that look of his that said I was a little weird.

Our conversation was sidelined as our daughter Slim came in with the boys. At age ten she was a big help entertaining them, which was no easy task. She had brought them from the babysitter on her way home from school. After the usual show of the boys' artwork, Slim was ready to take them for a buggy ride. Horses were her main love, and her small pony Pace was her pride and joy. The three of them never tired of Pace and the cart.

The Challenge

My friend Sybil and I spent a part of each day talking over our problems and those of the world. Her personal problems and search for a way to alleviate them led Sybil to books on various topics. I had no time to search. I had a sales-job. One day at my house, she had even searched the Bible for answers. Now, as I was getting supper, I vividly recalled the day four weeks before, when she sailed into my house, talking so fast I could not make heads or tails of her words. She told me: "Wait 'till I show you this!"

I looked at a notebook full of almost unreadable writing.

"You wait 'till you hear thoughts come into your head and then write them down. It's a way of collecting yourself and getting a direction. It helps! I mean the writing down of my thoughts helps. It's a way to get rid of things you don't want to tell anyone else. You can give them hell on paper, but don't mail it. Just tear it up. At least you've gotten the thoughts out of yourself. It's like washing out hate! I can think again and not choke up with bitterness. Oh, God,

Council of Angels

what a relief! Look, I'm shaking with the thrill of just telling you about it. I've searched and read so many books—to finally find something that can help is like finding a needle in a haystack or winning the lottery. This book tells you how to do it. I did. It worked. Now I can say, 'piss on it' and get on with my life. Those nerds that did wrong have a problem, not me. I did it right!"

I laughed, "Great!" It was good to see her in such a mood. I could only look at her in wonder. The last time I saw her she was l-o-w. Beat down. Today, she was bubbling with excitement. Some change.

She quickly continued, not seeming to care if I understood or not. "I found something in the Bible, too. I had written down the book, and chapter and verse when I was writing down my thoughts. When I looked it up in the Bible this is what it said."

As she read the words from the Bible to me I could only marvel that she got any meaning from them. I sure didn't. I couldn't see how or why those words could have anything to do with her problem. Obviously—she had received something which had changed her from a defeated person to one of excited anticipation. No way was I going to put a damper on that by asking questions and acting as if I thought she had lost it. But there was no need to say anything to encourage her to keep talking and telling me about her new find! She needed none. Words were spilling from her in a steady stream. Something had given her a new grip on life.

As she finished reading, she expected me to share her

excitement.

"Hey! Back up. Give this to me a little at a time. What's this about the writing?"

"I can write like the book told me to."

"Sybil, I'm from Missouri. Ya gotta show me. What book?"

"Just a book I read. O.K. Get me a pencil and paper. Do you know 'The Lords Prayer?'"

"Yeah, it's the only prayer I know besides 'Now I Lay Me Down. . . .' Here's a pencil and paper."

She sat with the pencil touching the paper.

"See?" Sybil urged. "I'll close my eyes and sit still. I'm saying every word of the prayer in my mind. Pretty soon these other words will come into my thinking and override the words of the prayer. That's all there is to it."

I shook my head in confusion, but sat quietly for a while, waiting. Nothing came to her.

She looked up. "I think maybe I have to be alone for this to work. Anyway, when it first happened, I ran into my bedroom and shut the door. After a while, I decided my bedroom door wasn't going to protect me and I went back to my chair and tried the pencil again. This time, I got words, wrote them down, and after I stopped writing, I read what I'd written. It was so peaceful! I couldn't believe how my feelings changed. I knew I'd be all right. I knew my life was up to me and I didn't have to worry about a dumb-ass husband. He'll have to worry about his own dumb acts. He has to find a way to straighten out his life, and I'll do mine. Maybe with him or without him, but it'll be O.K., and I'm not responsible for what he does. He is!"

I walked to the stove and poured a cup of coffee. "Gosh, Sybil, I'm so glad for you. Maybe I'll try to do this writing in the morning before anyone's up. It's quiet then. Do I have to read the Bible, too?"

"The book told me how to write. The writing told me where to read in the Bible. Try it."

I sure did try it as soon as she was out the door.

It didn't work.

In the quiet of the morning, at five o'clock, I tried again. No luck. It had seemed to work for Sybil. What was wrong? I was out of time, anyway, because Chigger was up.

Reaching Out

I spent many mornings with Sybil telling me of her experiences with the writings, and what they meant to her. She emphasized that she looked forward to the day instead of having to drag herself through it. The excitement of finding answers to mind-boggling questions via these writings had filled her quest. Her mornings started with prayer, meditation, and writing. To her, this was satisfying and exhilarating. The Bible intrigued her. She even understood the parts of it she read.

I tried again. Exactly as she told me. But I could not write. My mind would not be quiet. I had so many directions to go—doing household chores, fixing meals, planning my sales stops for the day and putting merchandise in order. But Sybil had opened the door to a new world. Heck! She really was a changed woman. Energy and enthusiasm had replaced the beat down defeated attitude.

When I sat to write again, for the umpteenth time, all that came to my mind were the many chores I should be doing; put in the wash before leaving, how much gas is in the car, remember to buy milk on the way home, be home by five so we can get to the school on time for Slim's recital. Carrots in the crock pot? I had better get on the road if I expect to be home in time. Give it up—not working.

I wondered how I ever thought the boys would be adjusted to our home in a few days. Bear was content and when bedtime came he snuggled down into a deep sleep. Not so Chigger. We were going on the seventh week and he was just as active and unruly as ever. I was exhausted. Most nights, while waiting for Chigger to go to sleep, I rested on the davenport the short intervals between rocking him in the big chair, changing his diaper, giving him drinks and rubbing his back.

This particular night, while waiting for Chigger to greet the sandman, I lay on the davenport watching the late, late movie *Hawaii,* a story about a newly-married missionary teaching his interpretation of the Bible to natives of Hawaii because he believed his religion was the only way to salvation. In the later years of his life he finally saw the Old Queen's way of love and caring as a missing part of his severely disciplined, hopeless way of life. Surely, I thought, he had given his life to God as a young man, but maybe not. In the story, when in his late 80's, he could see the Queen had so much and he had missed it. How sad! A life wasted. Then, I thought, I was baptized as a child and joined a church back then, but as an adult I could never recall giving my life to God.

So, in my mind, I thought, "well, if you're up there,

God, take it—take my life. See what you can do with it—I haven't done so hot."

Instantly, I felt I was in a whirl—actually felt I was moving; 'felt the sensation of riding a high ferris wheel surrounded by sparkling, bright colored lights; felt the thrill of being dressed up on Easter Sunday; riding my pony in full gallop; singing in a choir; beautiful music; my wedding day; my husband's love; a beautiful cool swim in a mountain stream just beyond a water fall—and all the happy times in my life. So many images flashed through my mind it was like a video in full color.

I lay there several minutes afraid to move. I was amazed! Dizzy! Frightened! Mystified!

When I finally got up, I went to check on Chigger. He was peacefully sleeping, the first time he had fallen asleep by himself. I quietly slipped into bed and slept soundly.

Coming to Terms

The tip tap of Chigger's little feet making a beeline to the kitchen awakened me, but the usual irritation was absent. I felt rested instead of exhausted, which usually accompanied Chigger's six o'clock trek to the kitchen. Today I could cope with it.

After getting the family out the door and on their way, I had time to think of my experiences. On the couch last night—that whirl through life—was that my imagination? No way. Not even my wildest imagination was that good. Something about that was life-changing. Still, I couldn't talk to anyone about it. Not even Sybil. Art would think I was balmy.

It was on Wednesday afternoon when I finally wrote again. I immediately thought, 'Gotta be careful who you tell these things to. A few days earlier, when Sybil had told an acquaintance about her writing and some of the wisdom of the words, the woman immediately decided Sybil's writings were from the devil and could only be evil. That included anyone else involved. That meant me.

Sybil and I reviewed the writings she had done—and discussed the many times we were referred to the Bible and how Sybil had received so much good. She had found a way to cope. A peace of mind so she could make it through each day—and night. She was no longer depressed to the point of suicide. We decided the woman was mistaken and unfair because she didn't understand. How could the writings be evil when they had been so helpful to Sybil?

The woman's answer to that had been, "Satan is a great deceiver."

Our answer, to her answer, was, "God is greater than Satan. God is the greatest." This is what we would cling to. After all—this was our only help. We had Bible verses to prove God was the greatest.

"'Romans 8:31: If God be for us, who can be against us?'

"'Romans 10:13: For whosoever shall call upon the name of the Lord shall be saved.'

"'Romans 8:38: "Nothing shall be able to separate us from the love of God, which is in Christ Jesus, Our Lord."'

Studying the Bible was new to us, but these simple sentences we accepted as truth. This was the best we had and we wanted to hang on to it. After all, it wasn't new to be criticized. We weren't going to let this woman defeat us so easily. She didn't know our problems and frustrations and the help Sybil had received. Not only Sybil, really. For my life had been changed, too, through sharing Sybil's writings.

In recalling one of the first life-changing messages Sybil had written, I smiled. It seemed so long ago! She and

Council of Angels

I had been using our usual low-life lingo in discussing our problems and she suddenly wrote the following.

For one to cloud their surroundings with the use of profane expression is to enclose oneself within a mass of dust particles thus walling out their inherent goodness. These actions serve not a purpose profitable to mankind.

The shock of reading those words was an eye-opening experience. We sat speechless—staring at each other a few seconds. Then Sybil gasped, "No shit!—oops!" She had slipped back into that low-life lingo. Hard to change bad habits, but we were both working on it.

Jo Long

A Crash Course

Three days later, on May 25th, I tried to write again. Art and Slim had taken the boys as they went to school. The house was quiet. I sat in the same chair with pencil and notebook and said "The Lord's Prayer" 'till my pencil began to move.

Then, deep inside of me, I heard the words:

Words will come to you this date you will not believe. Go into the world and do my bidding. There is more to your life if you will let there be. Accomplish your small tasks so they will be out of the way for bigger things. You will have the strength to do this and the joy in your heart and the smile on the face, for you are happy where you are. Your soul will find itself here in accomplishment. Go forth and lead lost souls to fulfillment of earthly deeds. Best to know that you can lead. There is a way, with cheer and good will. They will follow. Oh so many hours of waste for the body. Heal thyself for thou have the ability. Do not dwell on the unhappy things. They are your enemy. Happiness is your friend. So be it. Go.

Council of Angels

Sybil and I compared our writings. Sybil often wrote of worldly affairs, different countries and their turmoil—sometimes predictions of the future. This encouraged us to search the world maps and pay more attention to the news on TV and in the papers. Politics was also opening new ways of thinking and entered into our discussions.

My writings were more about immediate home life. The gentleness of parents and grandparents, how each played their role, and the importance of each. Even to the extent of helping me with household chores, planning my day's work and how to enjoy doing it. The necessity of the small tasks like washing dishes, cooking and making beds and the pride when accomplished.

I was the active type and learned by doing, not reading. But the writings were so important to me I actually set a time—a special time—set aside for that purpose. After the family left for school and the house was quiet, I sat in the same chair, with the same pencil and with the same notebook. I prayed "The Lord's Prayer" until I heard the words in my left ear. It almost seemed as if someone was sitting on my shoulder. The sound came clearly. It was different, yet the message was clearly said. The peace, confidence and untangled thoughts that came with the writing were awesome. Often I could only sit in amazement for several minutes following the experience. It was of little importance that I hadn't understood all the words. I had learned there would be a time of need and I would then have the understanding to cope with the situation.

May 29, 1974

Come many timely deeds. The most of these unthought out but, nevertheless, we find ways to do them. Now how do you fathom the task before you? Will you postpone on and on or are you willing to attack it now? I will be your accomplice—go—together we will acquire recognition for a work well done—up.

I didn't try to figure out what they meant. I felt so much better after writing—what more could one ask?

My short hours at night were still wearing me down. Chigger still averaged three to four hours sleep each night and I felt draggy in the mornings. I felt the urgency to make sales each day, yet my housework was a necessity. Even with cooperation from Art and Slim, the daily tasks were becoming more and more difficult to get done.

Since school had started, I usually went to Sybil's house on my way to a distant city to make my direct-sales route. We needed each other. Our visits were a break in the routine as well as the companionship of sharing our writings.

I loved my direct-sales work, yet my legs were so tired I had to force myself to get started. The suitcases with my merchandise were getting heavier and heavier. My weariness was cramping my sales; I found myself going to sleep while driving on the road! This was dangerous. I was needed. I must get it together!

May 31, 1974, I wrote:

Justice in your life span will find its place with the aid of small human beings. We are here waiting a development which you cannot comprehend. Nevertheless, it will come to pass. Dwell not on transgressions, they are only self consuming, but look forward with a smile for all is well as it should be. Transgress not on fellow man. Their sins are small. Go forward unto better and bigger endeavors. I will show you the way. Gladness of heart, trusting of soul, accomplishment is yours. Final.

Jo Long

Practice

My friend Pearl, who was in the direct-sales business with me, was coming to spend two days. I was really looking forward to working with her and sharing my writing experience with her. I could tell her everything. We had been friends in high school, and over the years our friendship had grown. We could complain, criticize our loved ones, and ridicule ourselves, but the other would know what we were really saying—clearing the air, yet loving them still. She and I had a special rapport. She could help me figure this thing out. She wouldn't say I was ready for the funny farm. She knew how I talked and wrote, too. To write words so unfamiliar to me and the way they were placed—yes, she would know. She would know these words and properly sequenced sentences were not of my making.

I felt hurried to get my housework done before she came. Still, I took time to write.

June 10, 1974

Just these wee tasks you must fulfill. Are they so great?

Council of Angels

Together we will attack them all. Tempt not and expect not and reap all in way of success. These things that appear tremendous are not. Do not make them so. Action is the answer so be it to move mountains—only faith and action as you'll see. Take your friend's hand and guide her to us— we are always waiting such comings. Let's forge onward and upward to many rich rewards together. You are always in a state of upset. Ahhhh—Lack of faith in self and me. Why do you rebel so? Look up and smile. Enjoy those small things and fail not to see and set goals. They will work out. You have the aid of many, so fly ahead and never look back. Our way may not seem adequate but is truly complete. Stay on course.

This may not seem earth shattering, but to me, it was absolutely astounding. What was even more so, as the morning flew by, was my ability to get everything done in an easy, even thrilling, way.

The boys' case worker had appeared on time (a small miracle), and they were eager to go with her. There was no fuss from either of them. Nor were there critical remarks.

By the time Pearl arrived, I had my merchandise in the car, house tidied up, supper in the crock pot and the electric oven. I was ready and eager to be on the road to our first appointment. We needed to make enough money to pay both of us for the day's work.

It was after midnight when we returned home. We had cleared over three hundred dollars, a satisfactory amount. I had told her about the writings, but now she was ready to see what I had written.

After I made hot chocolate, we went to the living room and sat together on the couch so I could show her my notebook and explain what I had experienced. I watched her face as she read, trying to read her thoughts.

"Well," she said as she read the last entry. "For sure, this is not from you. There are words here I have never heard you use. And this is not the way you talk."

"I don't even know what most of those words mean. Some don't make sense to me. That's the way Sybil's is, too, at times. Later, when she needs to know their meaning, it seems to come to her."

"How come you spell shall with an 'e'? Shell is a sea shell, isn't it? I've never seen it used like it is here."

"I know. At first I thought I'd misspelled it. But the next time the word came up, I couldn't write it any other way. If I didn't put it down that way, I'd not get any more words. When I wrote it down, 'shell', more words continued."

"You mean you get this one word at a time?"

"Yeah, and at the right speed, too. That is, after the first time. The words come as I write them."

"Do you think you could write now? I'd like to see you do it."

"I suppose so. I'll get my pen and we'll see." I had started using a pen instead of a pencil so I could see it better and it would last longer.

I held my pen touching the paper and started to say the "The Lord's Prayer." Before I had finished the first sentence of the prayer, the words came into my ear.

Mostly has this been a day of success. What say you?

Are you not pleased? One task completed. Good. Rest. Tomorrow repeat one more task. Ask not too great a number for a day. Acquaint yourself with resources to build a sufficient store for future use. Hence will your days accomplishment be added to a fold and grow to a mountain top. Reach out for each day's tasks to bring an added joy. These other things which are wee tasks are being solved so no worry to you. Thus is accomplishment achieved to success. Sincere.

Pearl took the book and read. She had been reading as I wrote. Now she said, "Well, I don't believe this comes from your subconscious mind, either. I think it must be God."

"But, Pearl, I don't even go to church now. Nor do I feel religious. I've gone to several churches in my time, but it seemed to me I didn't find anything special. In high school I belonged to a very active youth group. Never missed a Sunday. We read the Bible from cover to cover. Really studied it. Each week we had several verses to learn. That is the only time I have been a faithful follower. Many times since, I have wanted to go to a church, felt the need—but, like now, which one?

Pearl read aloud from the notebook: *Just as near as your heart is to God and the abundance of love for your fellow man is the way to judge a wedge of interest in a location. Only those who find a true reason for life are they who seek an answer to the actions they do not understand.*

Through you we have reached another soul and through her yet another and another shell be reached. Can you not rejoice at this and yet you ask, 'Where is the church?' It is in the heart and the soul of all and each. The house of God is where you find it—only of wood and brick is the one for all the world to see as a sign of each nation's belief in God—not in man himself.

We read this many times. Discussed each part. Pearl said, "What is a wedge?"

"I don't know. We used to put a wooden, three sided wedge under a wheel to keep the wagon from rolling. I've never known any other."

Pearl said, "Ask."

"My gosh, I've never asked anything. Just wrote what I was told. We'll try."

I wrote on the book, "What is a wedge as you refer?"

A very clear voice answered in my ear immediately.

The distance your interest will travel from your heart. A wedge can encompass all. Only a small piece is a huge piece if it is love. In a modest case one may not think of the universe. It is a conception. Rest.

We were smitten with awe. Speechless. The answer came so readily. Pearl asked, "Why, if the answer is so simple, can't more people see this?"

Again, the answer came quick and clear.

They have eyes for amount and beauty and comfort of material, earthly things. The worldly body takes much time and it is easy to lose the true meaning of life. Only when one does find him time can it be given to him a understanding and thus tranquillity.

We sat quietly for several minutes until I said, "I'm

amazed."

Pearl said, quoting the Bible, "There is a time for all things."

Immediately, I heard: *And each shell come at its own time unto you.*

Pearl said, "God shall provide, yet the Lord helps those who help themselves?"

Meaning—he who asks shell receive. He who asks abundance shell perish.

We asked, "How do we say 'thanks'?"

Again, and immediately came: *Thanks is not necessary—our joy is complete. Joy! Joy! Joy!*

At the time, when I was writing the joys, came an overpowering feeling of—something! Pearl and I both felt it. So filled were our hearts that tears came to our eyes and rolled down our cheeks. We were caught up in wonder, thrill, awe; a breathless, full feeling. At the same time we both said, "Love."

It engulfed us. The room was full of it. We knew the faults of our loved ones and each other, and we knew God knew our every secret, shortcoming, and failing. We needed to make no excuses for we were still loved and with no if's. Simply, it was. Our love was great. But this was a different type of love never before experienced by either of us. The feeling made us dizzy and lightheaded. Every pore of our body was saturated with it.

This was unconditional love.

With Pearl's visit we had discovered we could ask questions and receive answers and much understanding.

The next morning, before Pearl left for her home, we had to write more. I started the only way I knew, with "The Lord's Prayer" and concentrating on it to the extent I saw each letter of each word in my mind's eye, until I heard the voice loud and clear in my ear.

Put this day on record as success already. Pure of heart, staunch of faith. Excitement will pass but deeper understanding will grow. Ask questions if desire.

I asked: "Why do I want a better house if it is of no deep meaning? Let me tell you here, that we live in a small, two-bedroom home that needs remodeling. It is not impressive. It is warm, homey, and adequate."

Be ye judged by earthly beings a success or failure by the abode in which you dwell. Of no significance is it to us.

"Should it be of importance to me what earthly beings judge?"

Yes. For in their eyes they will follow your footsteps or seek other ways which are of fruitless flavor.

"What do you mean 'fruitless flavor'?"

That which is good has a savory taste. Fruitless has no flavor.

We giggled at the way of the speech but found it delightful.

How can we achieve an abode that will do earthly beings benefit or one that makes them want to follow?"

By the walk of days you build. This is not clear? Well, then, they see happiness as each day comes and can see the improvement at each day's end. Oh! The beauty that will grow because you know it is so. Your heart runneth

Council of Angels

over with gladness. Ye of little faith bide—your time of reckoning is coming. There is no great need to hurry, you are near us already. The love that has wedged out has engulfed you. You are near the heart. Only God can encompass. It is adequate. Meaning is clear is it not?

The feeling of the night before crept over us. It was as being in a soft, warm blanket. We could only look at each other and marvel at it. We were excited with such a find. It was a quiet awe filled kind of excitement. We could only sit and absorb it, too filled with overwhelming reverence to move or disturb this loving feeling in any way.

As we gradually regained our normal selves, Pearl commented, "God. This can only come from God."

"We can actually hear from God? This is far beyond anything I have heard in any church."

"What have you thought God was?"

"I never thought about him as actually being. Certainly not able to contact anyone. He was like the Empire State Building. Big. Something respected, but not active—like a myth way back when. What about you."

"I believed there was a God, but not for now. Maybe some time in the future He would come to earth from outer space. Like you, I have never thought of him as active in any way. Not really dead, but just way out in space somewhere. We called it Heaven. I always wondered just where Heaven was. We can ask—why don't you ask?"

"What will I ask?"

"Anything. So we can learn something."

I started my prayer and quickly came the words:

A process of growth in life dimension by the measure of which is a gram of perfection and understanding of others of all ages. It is never a complete thing in one life but an accumulation of many. Profit from each day's learning and put it to a good use to those near you. They are the lambs of your salvation. To put in a more meaningful phase—a way to lead leads you first to salvation and helps them on their pathway.

"Well," I remarked. "What do you make of that?"

"Positively none of that came from you!"

"No argument there. Let's see about down to earth things. I'll ask, "What can you tell me about my sales business?"

This is a way to reach out to others as you have said. But in it see a guideline to lead—not follow—as these you come into contact with are on a slower, lower pathway. Do not desist—it is as it should be. Do not enter it deeper as it is for the worldly achievement we spoke of. Nor do not belittle it. All accomplishment must have meaning so be it a successful meaning. It is times of stress by which we are measured and the condition in which we overcome each obstacle that matters most. Your sales give you new fields to conquer. Children keep your love and understanding on a simple level. Thus can you see they go hand in hand to one another.

A friend is a friend in heaven. A love is everlasting. Be not hasty in the choices for they are many. Put each in proper place and go onward up life's pathway. Oh happy days of rejoicing when we reach heaven's gates and are greeted by reaching hands of love. They are overjoyed as are you with such a reunion. Many things to learn.

"Gee whiz! After all of that writing you'd think I'd have writer's cramps. My hand and arm are fine. In fact, I can write more."

Pearl sighed. "Boy! There's a lot here. But, 'higher pathway, lower pathway'? How about 'lead you first to salvation'? I thought salvation was only when you were dead. Is that what it means?"

"I don't know. I don't know what salvation is. What about these other words—'life dimension, faith, blessed, gram of perfection.' Then way back here are words like 'sanctify, soul, divine power, redeem, and atonement' which are all new to me. I've no idea what they mean."

"Is there a dictionary in the back of your big Bible?"

"Yeah, here it is. What first? Well, here's this one. 'Sanctify: separate from the world and consecrate to God.'"

"Where did you get that from?"

"Back here, where I wrote: *Mother sanctify thy being by telling of the faith in our souls everlasting and look up for guidance from a divine power you must recognize as your proctor and guide.*

"I underlined all these words that were new to me."

Pearl pulled out a pen. "Well, let's see what they mean. Give me the words and I'll look them up. You write the meaning down."

The meaning of each word gave us renewed enthusiasm.

We thought we knew the meaning of some of the words, but as we searched we discovered our meaning was different. Like trust. The only trust I had been acquainted with was in trusting your husband, boyfriend or business partner. As for guide, I knew it only as a fishing trip or through the mountains. Now these words had new meaning to us. My outlook on life was growing broader.

Pearl began laughing and teased, "Hey! you've come a long way. From writing a letter once a year and reading a western once in awhile, you're using words you never heard of and writing every day.

"Yeah, who'd a thunk it?"

After Pearl left, I quickly went through my house chores in sort of a fog, buoyed by memory of our experience, and in the back of my mind was the thrill and expectations of the next time I could write.

I was still intoxicated with the wonder of it.

Family Matters

On the weekend our oldest daughter came with her family. Nell wanted to see an example of the writings, as had Pearl. As a college student I was sure she would be a good person to come up with interesting questions. After I got started, I told Nell to ask questions.

"What are we to ask for?"

Quickly I heard the words in my ears.

Nothing. Your heavenly father knows your needs.

"Why am I so scared?"

He who knows not fears what is to be.

"My faith is not strong enough. How can we become sure of our faith?"

By looking upward and keeping His word. He will lead you to life everlasting.

"Is it possible to keep His word?"

Mankind is made to sin and overcome each ultimate task set before him. He cannot reach perfection of purification in a day. Mistakes are expected but let them serve you. Go in peace for the Lord is with you always. You have only to ask and ye shell receive Him in your heart. Are you not joyous the Father is at hand?

Nell looked at me, clearly confused. "Is it wrong to want and set your goals for certain material things?"

No. For each goal is a milestone on your pathway to eternity. The larger the goal the greater the distance traveled.

"Can this be toward heaven when we set our goals for material earthly things?"

Yes. It is not the goals of earthly articles you are judged on, but the manner in which you achieve such. Goodness of heart, temperance of living, thought of those around and near you.

"Again, may I ask, why do we want earthly things?"

Again I tell you. For the sign to show the world the house you build is for the soul as well as bodily comforts. Can a day's treachery build a sand castle when mischievous ways are at work? So are we mischievous children of God when we transgress on fellow men.

Nell leaned forward. "Are you the original disciples of God taught by Him or are you souls who have lived and have reached a level?"

Both. As your needs arise he who can best serve to answer on your level will be at hand.

"Does one soul live many lives and at different times?"

Ahhh, yes, so many. So great is the work of the Master to do it takes many worldly bodies. Be gentle with yourself. To never have perceived and then long to be engulfed completely is much. Your questions are timely and good trend is the heart so that your soul is crying for justification. Search more. We are with you.

"There is so much to understand and there has never been a source before. Will I be able to do this? Will I find the right source to reach you?" Nell asked.

Search not for the source. It is given you. Ask and ye shell receive. Granted to all mankind is the counsel of the Father. Do you not listen when your child beckons? Is Your Father lesser than you? Then why do you doubt His counsel?

"I don't!"

After sitting quietly a while Nell said, "I'd like to tell my husband about this, but I don't dare. I wonder why it's so hard to discuss some things with the one you love the most."

"Well, let's ask," I said. The answer was already being spoken in my ear.

We fear disfavor and ridicule and we cannot favorably argue a point. Discussion is a process of practice from which we tend to grow away from if not actively kept up to date.

I asked, "Are you souls between lives or do you need to return to another life?"

We are at different phases of levels. Each level is a work of completeness with God. At our bidding do we choose the life we enter to further our souls' glorification. Not all of us have need to return to a temple of life to acquire the higher levels. Souls such as you are becoming more in number and our work can in some instances be thorough from levels.

"What has turned more people to you?"

Their lostness. For nowhere is tranquillity, and the swift changes that beset the universe are many. A soul will try in an earthly body and be swept up in worldly change so do they feel the standards of the universe must be updated. Not so. As it was in the beginning is now and ever shell be. The likeness of situations are as in your time and mine. Only worldly accomplishments are reshapen to achieve the sameness of the end. Peace.

"Are God and Jesus one?"

Are you one with your father? How can this be? In the love of the kingdom and the purification of mortal man are they one. Less than this is incompleteness. Glory to God in His Highness. He gave His only son for those who transgress against Him for all the world to see. Each of us know in his heart the strength this takes. To give a perfect image was the ultimate.

"Why do men cheat their fellowman, and steal what belongs to another?"

The accumulation of worldly goods is the only thing they can see to accumulate. Shallowness of depth of the soul is rampant and answers are not acceptable. They are striving for stores of plenty in empty bins.

A granary of hulls is of no use
A mountain star or woodland stream
Can be a fuller answer to a dream
A chant about a worthy man
Holds much more than a golden can
A monstrous deed; a snow white steed

Council of Angels

Are likened to a world in need
A golden fawn; a willow twig
Are so very much! They are big
A set of prints made so clear
By a lost mountain deer
Brings turbulence to drinking spring
Never again to be the same.

We sat speechless for several minutes after I wrote this. Nell said, "That does it, Mom. Whatever this is, it certainly didn't come from you. I have to believe it is from a heavenly source. No way did you ever write two words that rhyme. The answers are right on. What does Dad say about all of this?"

"It has him mystified. I can't stop telling him about what happens because he needs to know what's goin' on. He hasn't had me confined yet. Now, this poem! Well, he'll just have to adjust 'cause there is no way I can say it didn't happen, can I?'

Nell said, "Let's ask something else."

I wrote: Any message of learning, please?

This is a task that next needs to be met. A learning process of accepting God in the heart at all times not at only given times of one's choosing. God is at hand and awaiting acceptance. Ask and it shell be given. Go then into the closet and find peace of mind and soul everlasting. On our pathway reach out to the hands of friends at hand. This feathers the distance covered. We wait.

Our daughter and family had been gone several days

before I showed Art what we had written, including the poem. His remark was, "I don't know. Seems you get some good answers. This poem is a new thing. Maybe the learning process they talk about will shed some light on things. That 'ask and it shell be given' is something I question. I was taught to believe there was answer to prayer."

I told him, "I say 'The Lord's Prayer' before I write. Now, it seems to have a lot of value. Years ago, when I was about ten or twelve, I got on my knees at the east, upstairs window of my bedroom and prayed as hard as I knew how for my uncle. He drank too much. I really thought my prayer would change him and he'd stop drinking. Didn't happen."

Thoughtfully, Art told me, "Back in the thirties, my Dad was working so hard to keep his farm, I prayed for him. It never did any good and I decided prayer was no help. I quit praying. He was a good man, went to church every Sunday, lived as he was supposed to—still my prayers were not answered. Why not ask and see what they have to say about that."

Here is the answer we got.

No, his prayers were not answered. They were recorded in 'The Great Ledger' and his soul was blessed. His father had crossings to surmount and trespass. Our heavenly Father knew his needs, but the son could only see the anguish of his earthly father. Fear not, for his father's losses were only of a worldly nature. He progressed here and has his name engraved in gold for he overcame, not only himself but his family. They, together, found tranquillity everlasting. He is here with us now and is watching the progress below.

"Are the names recorded in different colors to indicate the nature of the task completed?"

Yes. Gold is of the highest nature. Thus as it is here also is it there. Gold is the highest of value in your domain. Have you not wondered why gold is so precious? It is because He willed it so.

"Diamonds are also precious here—is there a reason?"

A gem in a crown of glory to shine for all to see.

"This seems like we're wearing our blessings for all to see."

Yes. All the world is encouraged by success and the light shines on them for encouragement and guidance.

"Then do we lose our blessing in heaven?"

It is not the same. In heaven the treasures are of greater nature. Can you see the mind grow? You are measured in growth of the mind here.

"What is the crown of glory you refer to?"

Select few receive a crown of glory. They have already progressed beyond your level and wear their crown for many accomplishments. We can give a crown of straw for tasks, a crown of silver is harder to acquire. A crown of gold is of the highest and one of many jewels we work for in many lives.

"Many lives?"

Yes. Many lives.

Art and I exchanged looks. He said, "I don't know

about this 'many lives' stuff."

"Well, neither do I. Maybe this is one of the things we'll be learning about. I know some people believe in it. I can't see how it's possible."

"Me neither. Have you found the word 'wedge' yet? That seems to be an indication as to the reality of these writings."

"No, I haven't. That causes me to question the whole deal."

"I think it's a local word framers use for a piece of wood used in splitting logs." He stood for a moment. "Well, I'm going to mow the pasture."

I was perplexed. "No way could I say these things had not happened. I wrote and asked.

"Is the word wedge in the Bible? I do not find the answers I'm looking for."

We will have difficulty with timely words. Look further.

Council of Angels

Doubt

The following morning, June 5, 1974. I said my prayer, then wrote: "My faith is easily shaken. How can I increase it?"
Your faith only needs reassurance and repetition.
"I want to write this morning but I have no questions. I am anxious to receive anything you want me to."
We have passed beyond the deep meditation of contact. Am I not with you always except in times of bodily duties? Go this day and extend to all thoughtfulness, understanding and friendship. Your's will be another day of peace and contentment. Reap the joys of the wind—drink in the abundance of nature that surround you. Speak of it to others.
"Why am I so tired?"
It is only a frame of mind. When the body is relaxed, rest.
"Is it right to ask for help in my business because I need money?"
Yes. It is good to want to achieve success.

"I expect help from you in my work tomorrow?"
I am with you always.

The next two days I was to be at Pearl's and work with her. My family knew Pearl and I enjoyed being together, and I was grateful they encouraged me to go.

I arrived at Pearl's before bedtime, and early the next morning we made our first stop at a nursing home. Much to our surprise we found three people we knew had entered the nursing home. We took time to visit with each of them. This made us have a late lunch and our list of business contacts was now met with conflicting time schedules. We decided to have a leisurely lunch and go home and fix supper for Pearl's husband.

While we were busy fixing the food, Pearl turned on the TV news. We gave our little thoughts about the affairs of the world, discussing many of the officials, their slight handicaps and poor judgments. Weighed down with worldly affairs on top of our slow day in business, we were losing our lighter attitude. Pearl said, "Why don't you write?"

I got my notebook and pen and wrote:

"We are ready to receive."

Oh glorious day of reckoning for your friend is at hand. She need worry not for the world, for man shell find his peace in the way of events. Faith in oneself, faith in higher guidance, go hand in hand to achieve the same end. Man was not made to diminish so quickly. A process of growth and regrowth he is made of. Now is a regrowth of betterment and from then a knowledge of learning will progress to the next phase of worldly events in the universe.

Timely, tho our progress appears, it is a page of eternity. The earth is a work ground for souls.

Give us thanks this day as we give thanks to others. It is not what we do but the way we do it. What say you—a day of enjoyment and contact. Did not everyone greet you with a smile? You smiled first—did you not? How then was this day's task undertaken—with good will! Not a smile to strangers. Is this not then the way to greet each and every day? You have left fellow travelers better for having touched you this day. This has been true for all day. Man is not meant to be alone. Seek answers.

"Should we pursue only one course in life? I mean, occupation or work."

It is a dull life you expect for a searcher but a very comfortable life for one who accepts defeat easily.

"What makes searchers?"

Their souls have reached an impasse with their salvation. Some start a task—never completing it, or as soon as a task is completed to their satisfaction, never starting a new one.

"What is salvation?"

Salvation is purification of soul.

"Will handicrafts help purify the soul?"

Any action that brings joy and contentment to fellow travelers can be an act of purifying and reaching out to heaven.

We were feeling the odd state we had experienced at my house when she and I were first writing.

Looking at each other with big eyes I wrote, "Will this strangeness leave?"

This you feel is my loving presence within you. Can't I be with you?

"How can we describe this feeling?"

By numbness of too much alcohol.

What shall we call you?

Be it safe to refer to us as the realm. We reign in a realm around and beyond. Yes, we too can enjoy our work.

"My Slim is so anxious. Can I be of help in her receiving from you?"

She is struggling—a guiding faith can be of help.

"I was afraid I may guide her wrong."

There is your 'little' faith of self showing again. You are the best she can see.

"How can I be sure these answers are not conjured up in my mind by my subconscious?"

Ha! Now—oh doubting one, you even have a sense of humor that heretofore has been alien to you. So make the next move. There is no make believe about this. Yes, we have fun, but we get work done—so there is a moon so is there a sun—never does one go down the other doesn't come up and shine on each their cast to bare. Go, ye, then to the quiet glen and be of help to child and men.

"What does this mean?"

Pearl shrugged. "If you conjured this up from your subconscious mind you'd know."

Council of Angels

"Is there a suggestion as to how we can help Slim solve her problem about her horses?"

Which problem? The people who have the horse or pony?

"They can both be solved?"

Yes. Move them. The place will be provided.

"How can I help?"

By putting your faith in me.

"That seems too easy."

Well, you certainly haven't found it so 'til now.

"Right! It isn't easy, but I promise to put my faith in you."

Pearl and I sat quiet a few minutes and I said to her, "Boy, opening the mind is a whole new world."

And the words came:

Opening the mind is more than a new world; it is a conception that includes the universe. There is no ending only tranquillity to guide you. When tranquillity is disrupted—back off for there is quickmire.

Now about the question of the pony. Be ye gentle with your daughter and seek her counsel for her heart is troubled. The ground will be found to feed the beasts for her heart will not still till the task is fulfilled. Sleep with a smile on the lips for we are sailing our ship to lead away this wee small drey.

When I climbed into bed that night, at Pearl's house, I was tingling with the intoxication of unconditional love.

The bed was warm and cozy, and I slept undisturbed 'til morning.

After breakfast, we thought to start our day with prayer and writing. I knew immediately that my source was different. The personality that came through with the writings had changed. I said as much to Pearl, then started to write the words that came to my ear.

My answers are more timely of sequence than the entity before. This is of us to be accustomed. Now, what next?

"Art has sores in his mouth. Canker sores. Can you tell me what can be done to help them go away?"

Rinse the mouth each hour with toxin fighters you can pick up today. 1, chewing gum of aspirin helps the pain. 2, mint leaves for sores of the mouth called wintergreen they have at the health centers. The oils of the wintergreen kill the acids in the mouth and then as he swallows this cleanses the throat pipes. Also very tasty. Well it is in two forms, 1 oil. 2, as your lifesavers. Simple.

"His back hurts, too. What can help?"

Now that creature only wanted out. This was said in my ear as Pearl swatted a fly.

Well, he has sprained his back—nothing is out of place. Get out that hot pad, after a hot bath and oils of massage. Let him lay with heat applied for about thirty minutes. Then sleep half a day and he will find those sore muscles will stop contracting on him. Next.

"My feet are swollen of a morning. Is there a quick help?"

Pick up those vitamin "E's" over there and take three—

Council of Angels

drink three glasses of water—then come back here. Go.

"I'm back and ready."

You want to know why I am with you. Your answers you were receiving were not clear enough in understanding for you to readily accept. Oh, you needed that contact, to seek out answers. Words we speak in each generation do vary. In older times they had a more flowery and beautiful conception of words than now. Your answers need to be quick and to the point to erase doubt. For this were you given me. It is good that you ask questions. 'Tis a certain level we can only sit on a rock and watch and wait. What next?

"What do you mean?"

We, here, cannot contact you. It is you who must contact us. We can only sit on a rock and await your actions.

"That seems a little much! I thought we were to do your bidding."

It is not I in the embodiment of world travel, but you. You are in charge of the body during earthly process. Your body is a motor for the work of your soul. You can accomplish much and some of the illness you have is not of the heart malfunction. It is in choices thus reactions of choices and progressions made during the living called 'life'. Choices are of free will. Reactions are set functions reflecting choices. They are not free will but firmness as day to follow night.

Believe we're going to quit on that. It's a lot to think on.

Not think. Accept. Terminal.

We had another day of slow, disrupted sales. That evening, again, when we returned home to Pearl's house, we wrote. Yes, we were disappointed with our small amount of sales, and to write always made us feel better physically and mentally. We needed some uplift.

No money except from one sale today!

Well yes, but think of the fun you have had ridiculing yourselves.

We were both surprised by those words! This was different than anything we had ever received before. The realization that "our source" knew and had been with us from the beginning of our day was mind boggling—even though we had been told, over and over, "I am with you always." Here was positive proof! For, you see, we had started our day by saying things like, "If I could only get out of bed at a decent time, "I can't get my house organized like I should, "Well, I sure don't get help, "I'm just too fat and out of shape, "I don't eat right, "I'm too tired to care." This had gone on and on all day. To have our conversation brought up this evening that was a shocker!

We sat there looking at each other, dumfounded for a few minutes, and then giggled like little kids who had their hand caught in the cookie jar. We were both feeling foolish and a little giddy.

Pearl said, "Oh, my gosh! Should we roll up the car windows?" as it thundered.

Immediately, I heard: *Don't worry about the rain.*

Don't be so apologetic. . . .and after all the health food put in the car. . . .search your book for answers. . . . Now!

Council of Angels

How about those pans?

Pearl laughed. "Oh! He was with us at the health food store, too. I told you I had a new set of pans. You didn't seem too interested at the time. Do you want to see them?"

I shrugged. "I guess. If it's important to you."

"I didn't know it was."

Pearl brought out a large box with a full set of stainless steel pans. We looked at them and then I wrote:

"We have seen the pans. Nice." But nothing came back. No words in my ear.

Pearl said, "Maybe I'm suppose to show you the other two things I have that are new."

She brought a new suit and a new jacket. Then I heard very loud, *Pans!*

Pearl giggled and said, "Maybe he's a salesman."

Smart. Smart.

We giggled, and then I wrote, "Is there a point you want to make?"

Yes, put those pans in your budget.

I have enough pans! Why?

It is the lead content of your cookware.

"But I have special cookware."

Put them in the trash. These will be worthwhile.

Now, I was really getting frustrated. I didn't want to spend money on pans. I pushed the pen and book to Pearl saying, "Here, see what you can do with this."

She wrote, "Did Jill write the answer to the questions about the pans out of her desire to own them?"

Are you both still so faithless? You are poisoning

yourself. . . . .

"Does Jill need these pans?"

Not just Jill. What an ego! Her whole family needs them.

I took back the pen and book and wrote: "O.K, O.K. But I still fail to understand."

Some of those old pans have chipped; they need to be gone, gone, gone. Do it.

"I have just spent $40.00 on health food. Are you sure?"

I am sure.

"O.K., I'll do it."

Will wonders never cease?

"Now what?"

Get those pans.

"When?"

Now! I will provide.

"I hate to get these without Art."

Is he your cook?

"No, but he helps bring in the money we spend."

I will provide. You will see. Take them home. She has them.

I quit writing because the rest was too ridiculous. I had heard, *Under her bed.* Now Pearl is a good housekeeper and I couldn't believe she had anything under the bed! I asked, "Pearl, do you have pans under your bed?"

"Yeah, a box to sell" was her answer. Then she added, with a twinkle in her eye, "Did he see the dust under my bed, too?"

I got a firm, *Yep.*

I frowned. "$40.00 of health food and $141.00 of pans—what will Art say?"

Give him some aspirgum and wintergreen. . . .He has the sores in his mouth. Do you? Store food in pans no more. You will have no need of the old pans since you have a full set of new. Chuck 'em out.

Ahha! I know where that expression Chuck 'em out came from—Hama. During the years 1953, '54, '55 that Hama, a Japanese/American, was prominent in my life. The expression of chuck 'em out was from her.

"Is there any more I should know about my cooking?"

As you cook, I will be there. Pay her by check. I said I would provide. Can I not be trusted this far? I am the divine guidance you asked for this morning. Get going.

"Well, Pearl, guess you have those pans sold if you will take a bad check."

"Sure," She said, "I'll hold it until you tell me it will clear the bank."

I wrote: "Operation completed. I am grateful. Is there more?"

No. Satisfied.

Arriving home I told Art of our adventure, ending up by telling of the pans. "If I'm to keep them, you can carry them in and open the box. Otherwise I'll send them back."

Art didn't say a word but went to the car and carried in the box and opened it and removed one pan. "There." He said, "Now we'll see how they are paid for."

While I got supper, Slim sat at the table for a long time, talking about her problems. She was pretty desperate to move her horse and pony. "Do you think," she said, "It would do any good to ask about it?"

I knew what she was talking about. "What are your questions?"

"About feed for the ponies, and shoeing and water."

I had no idea she had been so worried. "I'll try." I wiped my hands on my apron and sat down next to her. I picked up the pencil, but even before I could write anything, the pencil began to move.

It is being worked on now and we have put earthly powers in operation toward that end. Time—what is time if the task is done? Patience, Little One, the bird wings great distance in a day. A plane soars so high. The eagle roost is near the sky. Put your faith in I.

She need concern herself no more about earning money for a good purpose. We do mean the land shell be provided.

Wing your tasks in peaceful bliss.
The powers above will take care of this.
Out of the pasture will run your mare
Over the hill she will go somewhere
Of her return no one will know
'til the time for her to show
Now she will grow and grow
For within her womb will be a foal

*To romp and play each night and day
Along beside your wee small drey.*

Slim smiled. I put my arm around her. "Such a neat little rhyme. That should give you a hopeful outlook on the future, something to wonder on." It's plenty for me to wonder on, too. This always left me in awe.

As for Slim, it was obvious by her attitude. She was relieved.

A Personal Matter

One day in late August, Nell telephone me. She was nauseous. She was into her second month of pregnancy for their second child. As she talked to me on the telephone, I could hear the fear in her voice.

"Mom, why am I so scared? I went through the same thing with my first pregnancy, but it wasn't this bad. Please see if you can help me. I'm so sick, too, but the fear is worse."

I felt perplexed, far away, and helpless. She lived six hours from me. How could I help? If I was there would the fear go away?

"Oh, Nell. I wish I was there with you. Do you want me to come tonight? I could leave as soon as your Dad gets home with the car."

"I wouldn't want you to come all of this way every time I feel sick at my stomach. It's the fear. I'm so scared. Please, see if you can help me."

"Do you want me to 'write' and see what comes up? Is that what you're asking me to do?"

Council of Angels

"Whatever you can do, Mom, will be a help. Do you think writing will help?"

"It always has. I'll try and see what I get. I'll phone you back."

As I hung up the phone, I was thinking this is surprising as she had not seemed so positive about the writings the last time we talked.

I started praying and felt my arm tighten but no words came to my ear. I started my prayer again, slower. I was filled with anxiety. I saw, with my mind's eye, clear as a TV picture, a young, beautifully healthy girl. She had long golden curls to her shoulders and the air of feeling perfectly safe and unafraid—loving life. She was walking on a street of smooth rounded stones. Wooden-wheeled carts rumbled across the stones and the young girl was carrying a wooden cask to hold the beverage she was to fetch.

The time was late evening just before the sun set. The land was England.

A horse-drawn carriage pulled along side the young girl. Two of the Queen's men quickly dismounted from the carriage, wrapped a cloak over the young girl's head and put her into the carriage.

In a few moments, she found herself in a room of the castle, a well furnished room. Food and drink were available to her.

As night came, she was informed her duty to her Queen was to produce a child. She would be mated with four of the healthiest males so the child would be near perfection.

The young woman knew, after the birth, the baby

would be given to the queen as her own, and the girl knew she would be silently 'taken care of.' This was the queen's way of giving the king an heir—she was barren—and she would be saving her own life.

I felt chilled to the bone, and thought it was due to the experience, the feeling that I was seeing a land of cold and ice. One of rugged terrain, of robes made from animals and the odor of raw meats. The ruggedness of life was little more than that of the cave man. This was in the far north country—at the top of the world. The life of the woman was even more difficult than that of her mate. This clan was more affluent than the neighboring clans and was ever on their guard against invasion. The young woman's mate was the clan master. She was expecting their first child. At the first light of a cold, white day came the battle cry of a distant clan. Destruction was complete. Males were slaughtered, females taken captive. Women were few and the warring tribe needed to replenish their diminishing people. The young woman, now heavy with child, was taken as a mate to another master. Her plight was one of mistreatment. She was battered and subdued. Finally, she welcomed death before the time she was to deliver.

As this scene closed I realized I was being shown a different location, a different time, in a a different land. It was the cold time of the year, but the cold was passing into

Council of Angels

spring. The land was in the northern part of 'The Land of Shadows' The ice would soon be gone and the warmth of the sun would soon become reason to shed heavy robes. This day the tribe would see the water of the low lands where they would make their home for the warm months to come. It was a happy time.

The attack came as suddenly as a clap of thunder from a clear sky. She felt the shaft of a spear protruding from her chest as she fell, and her spirit separated and rose above her lifeless body which lay in the snow on the cold ground. She knew no more. Her horse stood guard.

I sat in amazement at the clarity of the pictures I had been shown, I heard the familiar voice in my ear.

For the understanding to pass on to your daughter, to quiet her fears, this life is to overcome. Her happiness will overflow. You have been shown the records on the Great Ledger. For reasons of great need for understanding are these pages opened. Oh, the worry that causes fear. Relax Enjoy.

I picked up the pencil and wrote:

The song of the bird
The flight so bright
Slight remnants
of gold
The hue of blue
Go mother again to be
Watch the flight
of the bee

Go sit beside your daughter's bed
Read to her, pat her head

The bliss of her kiss
Touch of her hand
Will fill the heart of
Any man
The sickness will go
As the small one shell grow
And bliss complete
Is yours to reap.
Peace

Still in awe, I picked up the telephone and dialed Nell's number. She answered on the first ring.

"I don't know how you'll take this," I started, fearing she would doubt such information. Here again, I had to share with her the things I had received, for I had no other way of offering her any help for her predicament.

She was completely quiet during the time I explained to her and read to her the things I had received. When I finished, the quietness on the other end of the line was intense. Then I heard her voice, small and quivering.

"Mom, I can relate to that. I can even accept it as a distant happening. I don't have to be afraid. All of those things are in the past. This is now. Thanks, Mom, that is a help. I wrote down the poem. That you wrote it is as hard to believe as the past lives you told me about."

My mind was whirling. She accepted those happenings.

"Past lives." I questioned. This was a concept I hadn't recognized.

"I suppose. It isn't present lives." Nell offered. "I can almost see the street."

"You've always hated the cold."

"Well, there must be something to it. I'm more relaxed than I have been for days. I'm not so sick at my tummy either. I wish we lived close enough to have a coke together. But, thanks, Mom. You've helped me. I'll hang up now. My fear seems to have vanished. I'll be O.K. I'm going to go check on my little girl. I love you, Mom. Bye."

I thought about my daughter. I couldn't say she was as reconciled to the idea as she sounded. I remembered her saying she didn't believe in reincarnation. I didn't know if I did or not, but that, I thought, may be my next area of investigation. I need to find more answers. I poured another cup of coffee and said outloud, "I'd better not tell Art about this one. Don't want to give him ulcers."

Routines

I'm sure, as you read this, it would seem my complete time was spent writing. Not so. Daily events continued.

Constant care of the boys, never-ending washing, fixing foods for the evening meals, each of us doing the work-a-day demands of living, including my daily sales business.

Bear was finding contentment and enjoyment in his new location. Chigger was the ever-present catastrophe waiting to happen. The nights were short. Three to four-hours sleep was all Chigger needed. Our evenings were a set routine of Slim taking the boys in the cart for a ride, keeping them occupied, while I got supper on the table. When others went to bed I stayed up 'til Chigger got to sleep—usually by 2:00 a.m.

How Chigger managed to destroy so many articles was a major achievement. In one evening he had broken the round on my antique rocker, slaughtered the remaining tomatoes, and demolished Art's prize nut tree. The summer had been pleasant with many fun things, but hadn't shown an improvement in Chigger's antics. Nor had we any pasture. I was getting impatient. I wrote, "Should we be looking around for land—a place to move the horses?

The time is not yet. We are moving obstacles from your path."

"Are we to do nothing?"

Right. I will take care of it. You will see.

I finally told Art of the experience with Nell. He sat looking straight ahead, "I think it's time for you to lay aside this 'writing'," he said. "You depend on it far too much. You're becoming a fanatic. I want you to quit it. Get back to your natural self."

Art was my equalizer. I did tend to go overboard on things. So, OK. I could put it aside. I wrote, One last time.

"Are there any parting messages?"

We will be here doing our work. Do remember the pathways that lead to the back doors of the cottages and use only them. We will tell you the time is at hand for other pathways to be used. Developments will continue. Do not fail to use that knowledge you have received for it is good and timely. At a later date you will be appreciative of the preparations you have made.

I knew Art was right. I needed to stop writing. Not forever—just until I could prove I wasn't obsessed with it.

I didn't want to hear him saying: "Run it in the ground," "Beat it to death," "Go over board." All of these cliches could be used to describe me, at times. I placed my book on the shelf, my pen on the shelf. I was getting life back to where it was before. No problem. I didn't have to write. I could make my own decisions. I could do it.

The rest of the day was normal and busy. But it didn't work out so well. My mind kept going over my writing and of the messages I'd received. It wasn't the same. I felt as if I had part of my electrical current cut off. I didn't give in. I left my book on the shelf, along with the pen. I was capable of making my decisions all by myself. By the time I went to bed my confidence was near normal. I was the same ol' me.

Go to the church and pray.
My eyes flew wide open from a deep sleep. What in the world? I thought. I was sitting straight up in bed. "Who said that?" I was fully alert. "What's going on?"
I froze. Realization came to me. I didn't need to write. I could hear anyway. I was aware of Art's rhythmical breathing. He had heard nothing and was in deep sleep. I slowly left my bed and checked on the boys and Slim. They, too, were sleeping and hadn't been disturbed.
I returned to my bed. As I pulled the covers up, again, I heard the other voice, but softer.
Go to the church and pray.
In much doubt, I mentally responded. 'What?'
Immediately came, *Go to the church and pray.*

"I don't know how to pray," I whispered.
I will guide you.
"Now? Or in the morning?"
At early morning.
"Can I sleep now?"
Rest.

When I woke up, the first thing I thought of was the odd message I had received.

How could I sneak off to the church and pray without telling Art? How could I tell Art? He thought writing was way out! Ha! What would he say if I told him this? Did I dare tell him? People had been locked away for less than this. He, above all others, was the one I wanted to depend on and whose faith in me I needed. Was this too much? What would his reaction be? How could I *not* tell him? He had to know what was going on with me.

All of these thoughts were going through my mind while I was automatically fixing breakfast and getting the boys into a routine. After putting the dishes away I walked out to the garden where Art was working. I said, "I have something to tell you."

He stopped spading, looked at me as he leaned on the top the spade handle. "O.K. What is it?"

"Something happened last night. At 4:30 this morning. I heard, *Go to the church and pray.* I was sound asleep. Hearing this woke me up. I mean wide awake. I didn't hear it just once, but three times. I know it's weird. I know it's crazy, and I know you wonder about me. I had to tell you. I need you to tell me I'm sane. I don't know what to do."

Jo Long

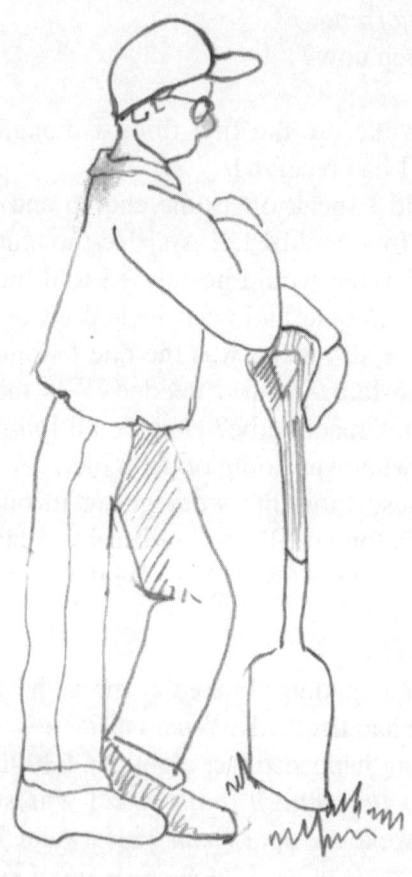

Council of Angels

Now he was looking down at the ground. He didn't look up as he said, "Maybe you had better go to the church and pray."

"I don't know how to pray."

"You've been praying."

"Not really. I say 'The Lord's Prayer,' then the rest is from them.

"Well, maybe you had better write and ask why you can't pray here? Why do you have to go to the church and pray?"

I went back to the house, got my book and pen from the shelf and wrote.

"Why should I go to the church and pray? I have been praying here at home."

It is a house of my presence. The message will be made clear.

"Can I receive the message here?"

Do as I say and understanding will come.

"Is it unlocked?"

It will be opened.

"I'm scared."

Do not fear, for I am with you and my works are within you. Be of good cheer for your husband is with you. Go unafraid. Feel my love.

"Is now the time to go? Because this is Saturday."

Hear the bird. (a blue jay's scolding) I am with you. Take the fear from your heart and leave only my love.

I checked on Slim and the boys. They were deep into the Saturday cartoons, so I slipped out the back door and walked to the church two doors from our house.

The church was locked. When I tried again later in the evening the doors were still locked.

Well, so what, I thought. Guess this isn't the way it was supposed to be. Maybe later. I was told I would be guided. Why didn't this work?

That night I didn't write. I left the book and pen on the shelf.

Several weeks later, one of my customers handed me a book and said they thought I would enjoy reading it. I was surprised to find it was one Pat Boone, the singer, had written. I wasn't much of a reader but I remembered him from the years on TV with Arthur Godfrey. I leafed through it before tossing it aside, but my eye caught a couple of words, "Faith" and "Holy Spirit." I wondered about these words and just what they meant. The 'writings' had used them, but I wasn't writing any more. I was curious about their meaning.

One evening, after Chigger went to bed in his customary wee hours and I was waiting for him to sleep, I started reading *A New Song*. Through this book I was learning the meaning of some of those new words. The next morning on my way to my first appointment, I knew I would find time to read some more of that book. It had me captivated. I looked for a park. I could sit in my car and read before continuing on to my appointment. I had about thirty minutes to spare.

At the edge of a small town I became aware of a cemetery to my left with a wide blacktop road leading into it. Large, tall trees shaded the area. It wasn't a park, but what the heck. I turned my car into the cemetery, parked under one of the trees and prepared to read. Much to my amazement, this cemetery was actually used as a park! Kids were riding bicycles through it. A couple of boys with fishing poles found their way to the edge of the stream at the base of the hill. Two lady joggers made their rounds on the smooth road.

I could relate to this book. My excitement grew as I read. No longer did I doubt my sanity. Others had gone through similar happenings. Boy! Was I glad to find that out.

By the time I put my book aside, I barely had enough time to make my appointment. However, I had several new thoughts in my mind and a new concept of what my writings were about.

I don't recall who handed me *The Cross and The Switchblade,* but it so enthralled me I completed it over the weekend, but there were many things in it I couldn't relate to. I had never been blind, so my sight couldn't be restored. I had never been deaf, so I couldn't have my hearing restored. Still, I couldn't lay the book aside until I had read the very last page. True, I had been more and more bothered with aches and pains. The Doctor had told me it was arthritis. I was becoming more worn out with our strenuous routine, but I was happy, and making enough money to do some of the fun things with my family, like taking them to "McDonald's" and "Dairy Queen."

By the time I turned the light out and got to my bed on Sunday night, I was thinking, I don't know about this prayer stuff, talking to God and having these things happen. That just isn't really possible. Guess I'll quit writing altogether. These books are for some people, but I'm different. Nothing so drastic has ever happened to me.

I was aware Chigger was up, of Art getting out of bed and going to the bathroom, of him talking to Chigger—and it was raining. Try as I would, I could not move. A slipped disc again? I didn't have time for that! The pain was too much. When Art came from the bathroom I whispered, "Art, I can't move. Will you see if you can help me up?"

As he came to the bed and reached his arms toward me, he asked, "What did you do?"

"I have no idea. I was fine when I went to bed. It's like when I had that slipped disc."

"That's been fifteen years ago. Did you lift something?"

"Not that I can think of."

Finally, Art got me to the bathroom and back to my bed. Tears streamed down my face and I was racked with pain. I took two aspirin and planned to wait thirty minutes. Maybe then I could get up.

I heard Slim and Art getting the boys ready for the

babysitter. I couldn't move my legs, roll over, nor move my position in bed. This was ridiculous! I tried to recall every detail of the past day but nothing involved lifting or twisting. Yes, my merchandise cases were heavy, but carrying them was not new.

The book I read came to mind. Now, surely, I could not have such a vivid imagination as to think myself into this situation. Oh no. I wasn't that good. But what if there was something to what was happening to me? Could I be in this shape just because I decided to doubt the idea of prayer and my writings? Well, I thought, if that's the case, God can change things back to where they were. I can get out of this bed. I can go about my business. I will accept this as truth, I thought, if you will let me get out of this bed and go about my business because we really do need my work.

I lay there several more minutes with tears spilling down my cheeks. The pain was excruciating.

Time passed. The pain let up enough for my tears to stop, and I could take a breath without wanting to scream. At last I could feel myself relax and I rested, in no pain, but afraid to try to move.

When Art got Slim and the boys out the door he came to me. "You awake? How you doin' now?"

"I'm better. The aspirin must be working. But Art, I'm afraid to move."

"Let's see if I can ease your feet and legs over the side of the bed. Maybe I can help you stand up."

It worked. Very slowly we got me into a chair. He handed me a cup of coffee and toast. When that was gone, it was time to try to move again. This time we got my clothes on. I was moving a little better and with less effort.

"You know, if you can get me in the car, I believe I can make it to the spa. I've not been there for more than two weeks, but I believe it's time to give it a try."

"Can you get out of the car after you get to the spa?"

"If you can get me in, I'll get out if I have to crawl."

"Yeah, right. You couldn't crawl this morning."

"Well, let's try it."

Very slowly and with great effort he got me into the car and I started on my way.

Before I had traveled half of the sixteen miles to the spa I *knew* this was the day to find a church and pray. I had no idea which church to go to. There wasn't one in the city that was familiar to me. A few weeks earlier we had gone to a wedding in a church on the far side of the city. It was a long, one-story building. If I could find it, I would try that church. Every forty feet, I thought, there was a door in it. Surely one of those doors would be open.

Slowly, I began to be aware of something. In my mind's eye, I saw a painter, dressed in a white cap and white coveralls. Glancing around the neighborhood I was driving through I saw no one in white, no one painting. I didn't even see a building that looked as if it was in the process of being painted. But as I turned the corner, I saw the church. There were no cars in the lot. That didn't keep me from trying. I struggled out of the car, but not one door was open. They were all locked tight.

I shuffled back to the car muttering, "what's this all

Council of Angels

about, anyway?"

As I drove my car back across town, pondering my sanity, I turned accidently on to a side street that was at a ninety-degree angle to the street I planned to go on. *Then*, I saw painters. Three of them. They were going into a residence. No help to me. I drove on, making a right-hand turn onto Main Street. Straight in front of me was a church. Tears filled my eyes and blurred my vision. I pulled into a parking space directly in front of a church. I had never been to this church before, but there was a painter—dressed in white—painting the front door. What kind of a church is this, I wondered. I looked up. Carved above the big door was "Church Of God." So, OK, it sounded right to me. I had never been to a Church of God, but there was always a first time. I wanted to stop crying so I didn't look foolish when I approached the church and the busy painter. I could not. The tears kept coming.

I got out of my car and walked to the front door. The painter's ladder had the door completely blocked. He looked at me and asked, "Would you like to go in?"

I couldn't speak because I was so full of tears. I just nodded my head. He said, "I'll open the back door for you." The man led the way down the front steps and to a small door at the back of the church. He took some keys from his pocket and opened the door. "No one's in the church. This will lead you into the back of the sanctuary."

I nodded, remembering the writings had said *By back pathways*, *Back door* and *Doors will be opened unto you.*

Pushing open the swinging doors dividing the back

entry from the sanctuary, I had a comforting feeling of being where I was supposed to be. I walked down the nearest aisle toward the front of the church. When I was about half way, I wanted to sit down in a pew. I turned to step from the aisle but absolutely could not step into the pew. It was as if my feet were glued to the floor. I knew I had to remove my shoes. This was silly. No where had I heard of taking your shoes off inside of a church, but I slipped out of my shoes, slipped into the pew, and sat down. Tears were still coming in an endless supply. I had no idea why. I couldn't stop them. To my left, I saw a light. At first only a small amount of light, then it increased until it was bright, like the rising sun or the sun of a hot, hot, summer's day. No heat—only brightness. From within the depths of this light I heard a deep, soft voice say, *In whom I am well pleased.*

I thought, Oh, come on, wasn't that what God said to Jesus when he. . . ."

Then I heard *Child of God in whom I am well pleased.*

I thought, I don't know what to say. Immediately, into my left ear whispered the familiar voice I was used to, *Chigger.*

I thought, "Oh, am I to pray for him?"

Again, the familiar voice whispered in my ear, *Yes, for someone has to care enough to pray.*

I thought, "OK, but I don't know how to pray for him. You'll have to tell me what to say."

I cannot record the prayer I received, but I know it was a prayer that put Chigger into the loving arms of God and from that day forward would he be in His care. Then came the voice telling me, *Ask for thy own healing.*

I realized speaking aloud was not necessary—only the thought. Through the guidance in my ear, I repeated, "God, if I am to do your works, you will need to heal me, also, for I cannot even do the small, necessary things a woman, wife, and mother must do. I need your help if you want to use me."

The voice in my ear directed me, *Read from 'Psalms' on the low podium.*

I thought, "I don't know where 'Psalms' is located in the Bible, but guess I can find it."

I stepped to the low podium. The big Bible on the low podium was open to 'Psalms.' I read and then I returned to the pew and sat. I heard from the light, *Your prayers have been heard and answered. Sing His praises.* I watched the light diminish as it had appeared. I put my shoes on and left the building by the back door, back to the painter whom I thanked. He said to me, "God bless you."

Starting my car I continued on my way, but I was so overcome with awe, I pulled into the parking lot of a restaurant to consider this last encounter. In the first place, I had gotten out of my car, walked up and down those front church steps, walked to the back and again, up steps and into the church *alone*! I certainly had not imagined the pain experienced that morning and on my way into town. "If I'm that good," I thought, "I deserve an Oscar!"

I sat for a long time, recalling each moment. I looked around. I knew I had to write. I picked up a calendar and turned it over. "I can write on this," I thought.

"What can you say?"

To go to the tabernacle was a need fulfilled. A step nearer to God, our father. Your prayers were heard and answered. Isn't the pain better? Now to the spa, to the healing waters, for your tasks have just begun. Go with gladness His miracles will be performed. Complete.

Art and Slim were delighted with the improvement in my health. After sharing my experience of the day we were elated, stunned, mystified. It was such an unbelievable tale, yet we were forced to believe. We had no choice.

That night, when I took my pen to write I heard, *Rest in peace for a task has been well done.*

Overwhelmed

Three days after I prayed at the Church of God for Chigger and for myself. I had improved an amazing amount. Not so Chigger. These last three days were a composite of all his destructive knowledge, plus. He bit the dog's tail, created more noise than any of us thought possible and broke treasures that we were certain had been put safely out of his reach. He seemed to be driven. When his inability to be quiet a single minute was at a peak, I took my book and pen into the bathroom, the only safe, quiet place, and locked the door. I wrote, "It seems we are making no headway with Chigger. He is extremely difficult! I thought praying for him was supposed to help? My patience has run low and my attitude is poor. I really need help. What can we do?"

Let there be peace in your anxious heart. Turmoil is not relaxing.

I wrote again. "Bear is neglected because Chigger takes all our attention and time and energy. This isn't right."

The very young are to try our souls. They are not stupid,

as you know, and although impatience decreases love grows—as it should—for obedience is a thing of learning and must be one of the first steps of growth. Is not your father in Heaven patient as with a small child while you learn? Do you not ask of things learned long ago? Improvement builds as a store of merchandise. For so long there is little, but soon the cellar is bountiful.

I hesitated before writing, "I give thanks and Praise His name, Dear Lord, but if I am what they call 'born again' why am I so depressed? I should be happy and tireless if I am *really* born again. Why can I not be happy? I find everyone hard to tolerate!"

You are concerned with worldly problems. Bills, finance. . .these should not be of great importance. They will be taken care of in due time. Look up, for all is well.

"Well, I sure don't see how 'all is well,' and our bills *are important!*—our renters haven't paid, horses aren't shod, we don't have pasture and the pans aren't paid for!"

I know. But still I say to you all is well. Go about your daily tasks for powers are at work for you to solve the timely bills. Be of good cheer. Complete.

"No, not complete! Are these last few days just my lousy personality or is there really a devil—and if so is he causing my troubles? Oh, God, you gotta do something. I'm at the end of my rope!"

Following me is not an easy task. Seeing and understanding are easy to follow. Following and seeing nothing and understanding not are contrary to the workings of man. To be my follower is of the utmost desire. To worry

Council of Angels

about answers you know not is fruitless. Yet to trust an unseen pledge is greater than anger and frustration, for faith is little used and trust is scant. Yet I tell you, your prayers were heard by the father in heaven and fulfilled by the mercy of Jesus Christ. The son and the peacemaker and comforter is at your side as your guide, yet, my child, you find it difficult to believe. I know your doubts and your tribulations and am in debt for services rendered. Be not defamed nor tainted in your faith for it is the true light. Frustration of small ones can be very trying on the soul but growth is a surety and the time of ripening is coming to a bountiful abundance. Songs of music are helpful at trying times. You will see some fruits of your faith soon and your 'little one' with love of lower animals will rejoice. Be of good cheer for all is well. Reap the joys at hand and lessen the strife in your life. A learning process of great importance.

"OK. Guess I will turn on music or sing. Anyway, I do feel better. Thanks."

After receiving this writing I felt better, really. But nothing else had changed that I could see. Maybe I was a bit more rested. Anyway, I had found a new attitude to help me cope with the rest of the day.

I came out of the bathroom and peeked into the living room. Slim and the boys were watching TV.

Art came from the basement and walked up close to me. With a frown on my face I looked up at him. "What?" I asked, perplexed.

"Do you know anything about the two kittens in the

basement?"

"No, I sure don't. Just what are you talking about?" I snapped at him.

"There are two half-grown kittens in the basement. I can't find any opening where they could have fallen or crawled in. They seem healthy. Call Slim in and see if she knows anything."

Slim was our animal lover, horses especially, and she had her little terrier dog as a house pet. Art called her into the kitchen and asked, "Did you put two kittens in the basement?"

"No, why would I do that?"

"There are two kittens down there and we're trying to find out where they came from. Do you know of any in the neighborhood?

"No, but there may be. How could they have gotten into the basement? Can I go see them? Are they weaned? What color are they?" With this she started toward the basement door.

"Wait, wait. I'll bring them up."

Slim stood at the basement door and waited for Art's return. He had the two kittens nestled in the crook of his arm, their bright eyes were as eager to see where they were as Slim was to see them. A few mews and the boys were there searching the sound. Art gave both kittens to Slim and she, in turn, handed one to each boy. Bear had the yellow one. It was more of a golden color than the usual dirty-mustard-yellow. The coat was so healthy it had a special glow. Bear sat in the big chair with "Goldie"

Council of Angels

snuggled in purring contentment. Obviously, this was a match.

Chigger took a death grip on the snow white one's neck and pulled it from Slim's grasp. She quickly retrieved it and explained how the neck was not a handle, that the walkers had scratchers that would hurt Chigger, and that the little feet needed to be supported. That white kitten was on to Chigger before Chigger could get his hands on him again. "Whitey" leaped from Slim's arms and hit the floor running. Chigger was delighted and the race was on. We watched the flight of the white kitten and Chigger until we made sure the kitten was safe. He was safe, all right, and could keep Chigger gleefully busy.

This game of hide and seek continued until bedtime.

Those kittens were the diversion the boys and Slim needed.

We made a special trip to the pet store for all the necessary articles it took to make the kittens house pets.

At night they were secured in the basement, as much for the white kitten's protection as to encourage Chigger to go to bed. When the kittens were put to bed, Chigger was ready to go to his bed, too. No more hassle. He slept two hours longer than usual. Those kittens were the best of babysitters. Their energy and patience were never exhausted. We were amazed that the kittens matched the need of each boy, one gentle, like Bear, and the other hyperactive, like Chigger.

An Island of Love

The morning following the arrival of the two half-grown, healthy kittens, I was wakened by the most beautiful music I've ever heard. It was crystal clear. The soprano voices of a huge choir, singing—like the crisp, clearness of a frosty morning

> *Glory, Glory it's a new-born day.*
> *Glory, Glory roll the clouds away.*
> *Ring the bells of Heaven.*
> *Listen what they say.*
> *Glory, Glory it's a new-born day.*

At first I thought the radio was on; then I realized I was the only one hearing it. Art was sleeping and if Chigger was awake I would certainly have known. For once, I was awake before him. That was a first. It was a very nice way to wake up.

After breakfast Slim and Art took the boys and I took advantage of the opportunity to get as much done as I could before their return. I was actually enjoying my house work. Dusting away, vacuuming and singing, I was shocked by the vision that came into my mind. I saw our family making a move into a home near a lake with a lot of open area surrounding the house. It was like seeing a dream in full color. Quite a perplexing experience. I was bewildered. Time to write!

"Now, what's going on? Do you have a message for me?"

Tell your friend of this little song.
Tell your friend to come along.
Tell her this is worthwhile.
Tell her on her face she'll have a smile.

Peppermint for bowels upset
Peppermint she'd better get
Not so much, just a stick
You will see a different chick.

This certainly wasn't what I was expecting to hear. I know nothing about a friend having *bowel* problems.

Was I letting my imagination run away with me? Did I want to move? How could this really happen? It seemed impossible. We had no money to buy a place by a lake.

Time is not come for you to know
Haven't we repeatedly told you so?
With God's plan comes happiness,
pleasures to man

For faith alone you're allowed to stand.
For trust alone your light has shown.
Following me as you will see
Things fall in place as it were to be.

See the oak tree on the hill.
See the daffodil—feel the thrill.
For thru us you've made a thrust
And found a spot that is a must.
Do not despair—trust, trust, trust
I thank you for fulfilling our needs.
It is not always for us to know,
But through faith God will show
The paths our feet should go.
Patience is a hard put task.
But to have is yet to ask.
The need is there for all to share.
The joys complete will be a feat.

"I'll go with what you say. Also, I'm asking for guidance in making the decision to go to Dallas. Can you help me?"

Just as always I am here. To go is to fill the thrill of a working career. It is no great distance, you will see, for I will be with thee. To learn of ways that are your concern, to boost you to the top of what you yearn. You will find a new spark to light the way of another leadership in much demand. To go is yet to understand the message you receive will be put upon a family love for with you will be their hope eternally. So prepare a valise of clinging cloth and soft, for a trip to be apart. On your return you will learn of the land you yearn.

"I'm thinking of the hardship on my family. I had decided it was too much for them. Are you sure I should go?"

Yet you hesitate. Yes. For what you learn will be of great concern. They are not helpless. Check your dates. There are ways.

"How much longer do we have to wait for the pasture? Days or weeks?"

It is difficult to move many people to accomplish our needs but when the time is at hand for you to know then you will see we have told you so.

"I've gotten away from my sales work since the boys came. Is it useless to work since there are so many drawbacks? My mind is confused. It seems I am divided in so many ways."

So many people you have met and so many more to yet meet. Go about your worldly task and make it a success. It is a source of money but also a satisfaction that shows completion of an undertaking. Continue to build your store but do not neglect to care for the ones you have as you have been doing. Concentrate on it and ask for guidance.

"I am asking! How to make it pay, keep my cool, keep my house and meet bills."

There is a way. Purchase a calendar. Place it in a place of equal access. Make a sale a day. Telephone on the wall. Use it. Now prepare your valise for Dallas.

Council of Angels

As Art and I lay in bed that night, I told him about the vision and that we would be moving to a place near water and that we would help many people find peace at that place for they would come visit us there. He was very quiet for a time then remarked, "Uh huh. They still haven't paid for the pans nor found pasture. Oh! That bed spring stuck me in the butt!"

I began laughing. He joined me, but said, "It wasn't so darn funny! That hurt. How did a spring in the mattress get broken?"

When I finally quit laughing, I informed him, "The spring was broken when we moved into this house. I told you they had a sense of humor. That's what you get for questioning their timing."

"You mean you knew we had a broken spring?"

"Of course I knew it."

"Funny I never felt it before."

"Yeah, it is," and I giggled. We both had a good laugh but could find no reason for the spring to gouge now, when it had been broken for five years!

Next I told Art about going to Dallas. His answer was, "Wait and see what develops. You can be ready in case it works out. Pack, like you've been told, and wait, or you may get gouged in the rear." We went into peals of laughter again and snuggled together in mutual delight.

A few days later I started the day with: "I ask your divine guidance for our family this day. Is there a message?"

Prepare your clothing—check what you wear nicely and start planning several comfortable outfits. Clean shoes.

Now. By the end of the day those outfits will be well on their way. Tomorrow still be of a determined mind for the wardrobe must grow. Sew, sew, sew. Improvement and understanding come with repeatedly listening to us. Sing—it will release tension. So many to put into motion and it is trying. Look up and smile. Do continue sewing and planning your trip.

"Why am I so nervous?"

Because you are going on a trip away from your loved ones. You do not know why, for in your heart you and your business are now apart. But I say to you:

> *For my sake this trip you make.*
> *For my sake do you your family forsake.*
> *For my sake do you your money make.*
> *For my sake do you your garments make.*
> *For my sake are these trips you take.*
> *For my sake are they too soon to celebrate.*
> *For my sake and no other are the trials you moan.*
> *For my sake alone are you to intone.*
> *For my ship will sail, His hold to fill.*

This writing left me more perplexed than ever. I only wrote: "Thank you for such a wonderful day and for such a wonderful family. I am so grateful for your presence. Is there a *Bible* passage to read?"

'*James 2, 18—24.*'

Another morning I asked: "Will Art look for pasture soon?"

Council of Angels

In time. By the sign will you know. Be ye first prepared in the home then of self—such as pants and blouses of the day, suitable clothing for the worship in God's house—make up for the face easy readiness of hair and items of care it takes and comfortable shoes of suitable types for your feet. Also for labors of fields have the clothing, for the toil of my land will be at hand. To travel far can mean an accomplishment of duty, not the miles to Dallas, but of a great distance as Dallas would seem to you. A near impossible feat. A good way to conduct one's life is in readiness—for only then can you do justice to the timely opportunities that unexpectedly come your way. Do not forsake me in the desire to reach out for a location to fulfill all your families dreams, but do be of determined mind to see this goal reached. Your husband and daughter are doing their fair share, so do not forsake the dream we have shown you. They know not for which they strive, so be light of heart and staunch of faith this place to brace. Home and clothing in readiness get—for til this task is filled will you and yours be thrilled.

See the oak tree on the hill
See the daffodil, feel the thrill
Hear the bird sing; hear the wind bring
Songs of happiness; smiles o' bliss
For rest not until we acquire you this
Go my child to rest abed
For tomorrow duty lies ahead
To put to order that home you own

Jo Long

Will be a small task for what we ask
And heart-felt joy as a toy
Each has longed for has at last
To reach is naught—to reach with God
man has for which he sought.

To be of prosperity is naught but to drink in God's gifts is as it ought to be. Grateful is naught if your help of mankind is not as it ought to be. On your door in the night will be the knocking of plight for you and your's to shine a guiding light. It is, as was Peter, a fisherman of waters, then of men, so it is to be a land on which to serve me. So many are lost and are struggling in deep water. Some will find a way to your dock due to your shining light and goodness of right to set their sails to flight after your guiding in the night. So, go. Be prepared for what at hand awaits your command. This is all I command, to be ready and on hand for it is on the highest land you stand. Rest.

I completed my packing and placed my two suitcases beside the back door. My housework was caught up and groceries laid in; refrigerator stocked with goodies and the cookie jars full. I was ready. I crawled into bed in the wee hours of the morning. I was satisfied I had completed every little detail. I went to bed in peace.

Green Pastures

I had finally established a routine of rising before Chigger and writing in the quiet of the early morning. This morning, for some unexplainable reason, Chigger, Bear and Slim were all awake and busily fixing breakfast in the kitchen. I joined them. Writing was not for this morning, it seemed.

As we were finishing a congenial, happy breakfast the telephone rang. It was one of Slim's friends. When Slim hung up the telephone, she was showing a mixture of delight and amazement as she told us, "That was Laura. She said the people who live by the river have pasture for rent."

Funny! Art and I just looked at her. We had all been wanting this information for such a long time! To receive it so easily was shocking. We were speechless. Art responded in a most unusual way for him. He said to me, "Maybe it would be a good idea if you wrote and asked about this."

I reached for my notebook lying on the table, and wrote: "Is this the pasture we have been waiting for—the one where the horses will be?"

By the sign you will know. I told you so!

No doubt about the three of us being in shock. Even Bear was aware of the enormity of the situation, though he did not comprehend the event. He only knew it was about the horses.

Art said to Slim, "Guess I had better telephone about it. What's the number she gave you?"

Slim handed him the paper and it was Art, the head of the family, who made the telephone call. A few months ago it would most likely have been me making the call. When Art finished the conversation he had that amazed look that Slim had had.

Art explained, "I got his wife. She said we needed to contact her husband who's at work at his place of business in town. She gave me the street address but the name of the business on the sign is Gregory instead of their name. Since they bought the business only last week the sign hasn't been changed."

No comment. We all sat there in stunned silence, remembering, *By the sign you will know.*

"She also said her husband will be there until noon today. I guess Slim and I will make a trip to check this out. Since we're all up earlier than usual, we'll have time to see about it before he leaves."

I waited at home while the two of them made the trip to town. To keep the boys and my mind busy, we made cookies. Bear and Chigger could help and then eat some. It seemed as if time would never pass.

When Art and Slim returned, both had big smiles on

their faces. Both wanted to talk at the same time. "We got the pasture!" was Slim's comment.

Art filled in the details. "This is unbelievable. The pasture isn't even ready yet. He was to put an ad in the paper today advertising it for rent. There's no water. The well diggers are to finish that tomorrow and deliver the water tank. The barn—

I interrupted, "The barn? There's a barn?"

"Yes. A large one. Large enough to put the pony cart inside out of the weather, store feed, hay and tack. Better than we ever dreamed!"

"But, can we afford it? What does it cost a month?"

"You won't believe this, either. For all three horses, barn, pasture with water and tank, and electric fence around the pasture he set the price at $35.00 a month!"

"Oh! Wow! Oh my gosh! And to think we were being asked $50.00 a horse and no barn! Well, a stall in a barn, but this is a complete barn? No other people or animals to share it with?"

"Right. And—it is one, *one* mile from here! Slim will not need to ride her bicycle five miles to get to her horses."

"Unbelievable! Wonderful!"

Slim came into the room dressed to ride. "I'm going to go see the barn and pasture even if it won't be ready for a few days. I'll walk unless you all want to come see it too."

We piled in the car and drove to the barn. It was beside the black-top road. The pasture gently sloped toward a creek but most of the ground was high and fairly level. There was a small grassed area to the right of the barn with a few big, old trees for shade and a graveled driveway where we could park. The feed way, stalls and old timbers were covered with dust, cobwebs and character. We examined it thoroughly and thrilled to every detail.

Truly, God was Great; so great he had a way of humbling us with His immenseness. This was a million times more than we could have imagined. The completeness was staggering. We could easily afford the monthly rent. The horses' every need was fulfilled.

That night, when I took my pen in hand to write, I could only say: "God, to know you is so great! How can I thank you?"

The joys of living are rampant. Extend the arms of love to all who come your way without a thought of malice, without a thought of pay. Pray to God in Heaven and thank Jesus Christ, for all the holy goodness is yours thru Christ. Take time to rest and enjoy God's gifts. Bask in His love.

We spent many days "basking" in His love and enjoying God's gifts. Slim spent hours cleaning the barn. Just being in it was a joy. She was in a heaven of her own.

At 5:30, in the quiet of the morning hours, I sat to write, and, again, say thanks for the provision of pasture and barn. I heard in my ear:

Put this way. How about the many words you read? Hunger for truth is to seek salvation. Many things you read are good. Many on the shelves are not. Leave them to rot. The truth is here in the hearts of man; their living Holy Spirit, but they know this not. With pen in hand we shall encounter to make this knowledge available to all who will

Council of Angels

pick up and read therein the manuscript we are to compose in His name. So, not the pen, but to a typewriter for more accuracy. . . .Do not cling so. I am here beside you. Paper will be found—together will be God's message made clear through you to your fellow man. Peace of the country and isolation of a house is near at hand His work to command. Typewriter.

I was thinking, "Manuscript is a book! Typewriter?' That would be noisy. I enjoyed the quiet of the early morning and clearly hearing. I didn't want to lose that. But I was told typewriter. We had a typewriter. By today's standards an ancient one, yet it did work, I supposed. No one had touched it for years and I had wondered why we still had it. I got it out, set it on a card table, and even found some of Slim's paper from school. I typed, "I'm ready, I guess. Let's do some practice."

See, you can hear me well. Must have this overhauled. Ok. Now down to business.

We are here for one purpose only—to perform for our Father and His son, Jesus Christ. . . .We will not worry about the outcome of the things we are expected to do but to do them as directed. Now is the time for books as the country hungers for information to guide them to their salvation although they do not know what they seek. Proceeds from a book will help fill out our plan. Information will come to you to be put to print. Working with God removes all selfish and central attention. His glory can be sung by many, His wonders to perform are countless and His praises sung by many men can be greater heard as each new voice is added. Go and prepare for this next step in your phase of living. We are moving mountains. . .so there will be complete harmony and enjoyment for you and yours.

> *Many things to be accomplished yet,*
> *but be patient and do not fret,*
> *For first to receive a knowledge is how to get*
> *The numerous tasks completed and aside will set*
> *A place of quiet beauty for us to get*
> *While tranquillity in your household set.*

> *Now hear the dove and feel the air.*
> *Where it comes from I know not where,*
> *Nor where it goes I do not care,*
> *As long as God's plan I know I share. Peace.*

Now, this was a little too much. *Me* write a manuscript? For crying out loud, a letter was a challenge. I shook my head. "Now, I'm to write a manuscript? Ha! when I tell Art this little piece of news he'll get a good laugh."

One thing for sure, the writing had a way of opening one's imagination to the fullest.

Council of Angels

....

Change in the Air

It was the following Friday evening when the boys' case worker came and picked them up for the weekend. We had not expected her for another week, but it really made little difference as the boys were healthy and could use the change. So could we.

By six the next morning Art and Slim had gone to help a friend cut wood for his fireplace. I was enjoying the quiet of the empty house and preparing for a day alone. I didn't have many of those. My telephone rang. It was Pearl.

Her opening remark to my "Hello" was "I thought you would be here by now. What's keeping you?"

"What're you talking about?"

"Didn't you read your mail? You and I are to hold classes in Indiana tonight and tomorrow."

"You're kiddin'!"

"I thought you'd pick me up on your way to Indianapolis."

"Pearl, I didn't know about it. No, I haven't read any mail. I'm packed for Dallas but didn't want to go. Art took the car and will be gone the whole day. Guess I can't go."

"Oh, no, you don't. They changed the meeting in Dallas to this one in Indianapolis. I'm not teaching that class by myself. I'll come get you. I'm leavin' right now. Get your pants on."

"I'll be ready by the time you get here."

I would have time to wash my hair and shower and dress as it would take her over an hour to get to my house. As I hurried to get ready, I kept wondering how I missed reading my mail. "Guess I was busy basking in God's gift," I said to myself. Oh, well. I was going to enjoy it. I would leave Art and Slim a note explaining what, where, and why. So this was what the writings were talking about. This trip that seemed as far as Dallas and impossible to get to. Right! The boys had gone a week early, too. Gee, how could everything have worked better?

It was a good, free feeling to be motoring down the road. Usually I was behind the wheel. This time, with Pearl driving, I could give all my attention to telling her about the latest events and about the pasture.

We stopped for lunch at a restaurant about the half-way point, and on the way out, I checked the books on the rack by the door. This was not my usual custom, but of late I had become aware of the many and various types of books.

One in particular caught my eye. The title was, *Power In Praise*, by Merlin R. Carothers. I bought it.

Pearl remarked, "This is something new for you, isn't it? Buying books? Why did you pick that one?"

"I don't know, just thought I was supposed to. Oh,

yeah. I'm to tell you to use peppermint to soothe your tummy."

"Well! How did you know I was having trouble with my pancreas again?"

"I didn't. I was just told to tell you."

The meeting that evening went very well and the following day's schedules were made. Pearl and I were invited to the home of one of the co-workers, Anna, so we did not have to go to a motel. Pearl and I had our own bedroom across from the bath. As we often did these days, when together, after preparing for bed we read the Bible. Tonight we eagerly looked forward to reading and then to writing. The writings said:

It is to praise, not ridicule our fellow man. Expect the best, forget the rest, and fellow man will pass the test. Then pray this way: 'Dear Jesus, deliver us from our sins, and show us the way to pure enlightenment for your sake. Amen.

And then say: 'For to you shell come my works that you show me. . .to be a work of my hands at your command. Rest.'

"Is there a Bible verse to read?" I wrote.

Be content with 'James,' any part there of.

After reading "James" we were not relaxed, and I thought of the book I had bought at the restaurant. We took turns reading the first chapter. It was about an alcoholic. We thought it a strange way to handle such a problem, but the man's wife praised the Lord for his affliction, and he was cured of his drinking problem. It was interesting.

I was dressing when Pearl came into the bedroom flushed with excitement, looking for the book we had read from the night before. I handed her the book and asked, "What's happening?"

"Oh, my gosh, Anna's husband is an alcoholic. We got this book for her! She really needs it!"

I finished dressing with new enthusiasm, curious as to the events I was missing. When I walked into the kitchen Pearl said, "She wants you to write for her."

Anna handed me pencil and paper and I silently prayed for help for the problem within this home, then I wrote three-fourths of a page and handed it to Anna, who read a small part of it aloud and then became so choked up she read only to herself. Tears streamed down her face and she sobbed, "Oh, how can I ever thank you?"

Surprised by her reaction, I answered uncharacteristicly, "Praise the Lord." I was curious as to what else I had written. I didn't remember any of it.

We left her sitting in the kitchen, drying her tears and smiling.

We had barely started on our way to the meeting when tears started to roll down *my* cheeks. I didn't feel sad, nor upset. The experience of writing for Anna had not seemed depressing.

"What's going on?" asked Pearl. I was as perplexed as she was. "I don't know. I feel alright. I even feel happy, but not hysterical. I just can't seem to quit crying." I was so choked up I could hardly talk to her. I could only sit there and let the tears roll.

Council of Angels

"Better cut it out before you ruin your makeup."

I knew that, but tears just keep coming.

Before we pulled into the parking lot, my tears stopped. I felt fresh enough to go into the meeting, but I worried about my eyes being red. Pearl looked at me. "They're not red," she said.

Pearl asked, "What did you write for Anna?"

"I've no idea. Can't remember a word of it. She sure seemed moved, didn't she? She was crying, too. She may let us see the writing when we get back there tonight."

We decided to sit in the car a few minutes, as we were only the third car to arrive. Pearl said, "Why don't you write and see what you get. Maybe it will tell you why you cried."

Hear this command. Go forth into the world today in much the same old way—unprepared. But see how much more will be the knocking on the door when you are prepared within. Put your heart and mind to this task, you'll find a reception of a different class. Reap the joys thereof.

"What do you mean—unprepared?"

Because of your failure to be able to witness for me.

"What is 'witness' and how do we do it?"

By telling of the things that have been coming your way.

"I don't think most will believe me."

Right!

"Then how do I become prepared for this? Guess you will just have to show us."

Our meeting was successful. The lessons were enjoyable and the people were eager and willing to learn. I dreaded the closing of the seminar which I was to present. I had been told by the writing the night before what should be said, but I was still nervous and queasy. I wished I could get out of the situation.

Just before the session was to begin, the manager of one of the organizations asked me if *he* could be allowed to address the group in closing. I was delighted. The shocking thing about his address was that He covered everything the writing had said should be covered, even to the exact closing sentence.

At the end of the meeting we returned to Anna's house. She had not arrived home from work, but had told us to go inside and make ourselves at home. In the entrance hall, just outside the living room, Anna had a very old, very large dictionary resting on an antique wooden podium. Since the writings had always spelled "shall" with an "e," instead of an "a," I had searched every dictionary I found for an acceptable spelling or a different meaning. I stopped to look in this unfamiliar dictionary. Much to my amazement it was there! The very last sentence of a long definition" "The coming of things yet unknown."

I was so thrilled! I showed Pearl and, she was amazed. Then she suggested we write. When she suggested it, I was always willing, although *she* thought of it more often than I did when we were together. So, I wrote, thinking we would get some sort of response about finding the word shell. I started with a prayer, "Thank you, Father for a grand day of friendly companionship." The excitement was so different than before. More quiet—assured of success.

So now can be shown how the ungreedy, unselfish attitudes of several people can be a joyful learning group. There are few who understand a friendship as you two have. Do not expect nearly so much from your fellow man for so many instincts are carnivorous.

"Can you explain?"

It is as if each quietly recognize the other's ability or inabilities and accepts them. . . .We cannot all have equal abilities, but each to his own ability. So is man made, but to rely on another's judgment and not feel you have anyone who has to prove himself, is where the quietness of personal self ability grows—not shows.

Now to go into another phase of living you will, both of you, find the guidance and competence of a worthy leader. It is not as leading a horse to drink. . .the horse must be thirsty—you only can open the gate and loose the rein. Move aside for he must learn his own self-confidence and use his own muscles, head and tail. Muscle is to motivate, head is to think of fellow man, tail is to brush away the small insects (yes, as an undesired co-worker), and all have the ability and instincts of reproduction. But each in their own pasture.

> *To flaunt a love is to step backwards, to reject a hand offered in friendship is to bury your head in the sand.*
> *To need not the comfort of companionship*
> *To give not is to become stale and hard.*

*To reach not is to sink and rot.
Man needs arms of love to hold him from the mire, for it is
too thick for him to live in.
As ye have done so unto me then let it also be
done unto you for the Father in Heaven
awaits at the golden gates
His promises makes.*

When Anna got home, we prepared a snack for her husband, her married daughter and family, as well as us. In a visiting, congenial way of getting acquainted we discussed many things. Anna told her family about the 'writing.' When she asked me what my writings were, I was baffled for an answer, so I held my pen over the paper and wrote:

*This is what my writings are.
Hearing God as from afar
Whispering in my ear
Many answers that I hold dear
Taking away my worldly fear*

*To tell the world about Him
And let them know
No one can do without Him.
Even the smallest task
Will be too grim,
Trying to do it alone
And without Him.*

But to have Him for a partner,
Nothing can be smarter.
For then things happen
Just like they ought to
And fall into place
For me and my partner.

The love of fellow man
Is something that you can
Because through Jesus Christ
All contacts turn out nice.

Go ye then into the world and do my bidding—I will guide you and prepare a time and way. To be of guidance to others, let's start today. To bow the head and pray say: 'Thank you, Father, for this day, thank you in every way. Thank you for the way we play doing seriously our work today. For these many hours together with friends and co-workers and leadership teachings we need so much. We humbly ask you to go with us each and help us to reach. For reaching is to God, to reach your fellow man and just help a little where you can—oh no—not alone, but with me there to condone, beside you I will be a silent partner and you shell see all things turn about as it were to be. Thank you, God, for being with me.'

The quiet that followed was as if we had been in a church and felt the reverence of God. We said our good nights and went our separate ways.

When I snuggled down in my covers at Anna's that

night, again, I started crying. When Pearl saw my tears, I assured her I was not sad, nor hurt. I grabbed my pen and notebook and asked, "Why am I crying?"

It is good-by to the old life and hello to the new. For to you will come a life of difference and a change in ways are a change in life .This should be a day of rejoicing for your light has shown, but to you was not known. My work is not done. . .so there is something for you to see. Your Father in Heaven is in control of hearts and souls, and each plays his role.

"Some people think each person has to pray for themselves. Can you explain this?"

Already has one assigned to him the Grace of God. Now for one to ask it for oneself is the expected and accepted. Why then how much greater a gift is the unexpected and loving gift. This is what you have given, for they are seeking and turn to empty paths. But you have reached out and handed them God's gift. You wept for they know not to weep and cleanse their trail away.

"Does someone have to weep when a person receives the Grace of God?"

Not always, for if a person is on the right path there need be no washing away of old ways so there is only rejoicing.

"Is the Grace of God always a good gift?"

Yes.

"But also the Grace of God is our comforter?"

By the Grace of God—by way of a gift from God each of us has the Holy Spirit—but if I have given you a gift of the greatest nature, can I again give you the same? There after God's gifts will be of many and various natures his wonders to receive. The Holy Ghost can be given but once, for thereafter the comforter is always with thee, within thee, of thee and His works are done by thee. Can you be rid of a mother who gave you birth, a father who sired you or the sister or brother of these parents? In no way can you be separated then from me for I am you and you are me. I my work will do through thee."

"When our prayer is for a person and they know nothing about it—how can we be assured they will be willing to accept it—for it is a new idea to accept."

New, yet old—since the beginning of time. For us to interfere in one's life is not of our choice, but of the individual or through the loving gift from another. Doubts and fears one has, if they do not know to reach out and rid those, for I tell you we can only sit on a rock and wait our presence to partake.

"You mean you are there all the time? Waiting?"

But of course. Are not the moon and stars there all the time, yet by light of day are out of sight of man?

"People don't know they have this type of help."

When reaching out in times of dire stress do they contact forces never before aware of. Many times due to dilemma they have found themselves in, do they reach for more.

And what do you mean 'the loving gift from another?'

There can be no greater gift than the prayer offered secretly by a caring person. This is a loving gift from

another. On this trip you have lit the right path and already has His presence been felt. From this day forward they will not be alone but find ways to atone for all the heartache shown and too will be so new a way of life that is too good to be true for those who are near will no longer fear but their voice will become soft and the hands gentle. Yes, quite a shock. Their ills will lessen, worries become blessings.

When does one feel the prayer? When they read the words that were written or when one prays?

When the prayer is formed. No written word needs be read.

"So very, very much to learn. Some ask what you are and I really can't tell them."

Read John. Tell them to read first John.

The next morning we left Anna's and headed home.

More Time to Write

It was good to be home after the thrilling weekend. With the family into their various routines, I found time to write a question.

"How did it happen that people failed to follow the Bible?"

Oh—you mean why doesn't man pray for his fellow man and have all problems understand. Well, one misinterpretation of written word. As of the day of Matthew—so began a new conception for the living man to put his faith in past works and miracles. This was the misconception. God is not dead—but for man to be taught so—then it is as if past a grave he'd go. Who tarries past a closed grave. A very few remember who is put to rest there for it holds no meaning—as a shell. But even a caged tiger stops more passersby. For the new concept of a closed grave to be taught by even those who were at one time in awe—soon the truth was lost at a great cost. For now we have to prove again that each has access to Him and that The Holy Ghost lives within.

"If my praying can help so much—should I pray for everyone?"

First is to truly care. How many do you think of that do truly care for another to be in actual turmoil and anguish for them? Next, is to pray through God and Jesus Christ for it is here alone they can come by their comforter. They will be humble when they realize the greatness there of. Have the home you are in ready to receive guests of the best nature. Clothe yourself to receive guests of great station. Only through Jesus Christ of Nazareth can any enter into His glory. Memory will be keen. With God's grace let's go to face the day. Embrace.

"My house is never done it seems, but improved. The book I'm reading leads me to questions. Can you tell me, is my writing a way of speaking in tongues?"

No. For it is not a foreign language, but direct contact with your savior.

"Any message?"

Be rested for tomorrow.

Sept. 10, 1987. Awakened by a blue jay at 5:00 a.m.

I showered, dressed, and put on my make up. This is the day I am to be ready for company. Chigger is sleeping later than usual. Could it be he's finally getting settled in after all of these months? I'll not knock it. I'll take advantage of it and write.

The morning was crisp, clear, with the promise of fall in the air. Settling into the comfort of my chair with pad

Council of Angels

and pen I bowed my head in prayer, "Thank you, Father, for this day and be beside us as we play. Stay ever our woes and feather our path with your loving ways. Amen. "Is there a message for me?"

It seemed a cool breeze came from—somewhere causing me to feel a chill. Then I heard:

Only of my doing is done this day. For it is on this day you will hear me say, 'Come, we have found a new way.'

Oh, oh. Something was wrong here. The personality was not the same. Something about it was different. This voice was youthful, lilting.

Follow me. I will give you the world.

I actually felt the thrill of night life, a richness of silks and dress finery, the party life of youth, non-caring, no responsibility; a freedom like 'Tinker Bell' in the nursery story. The voice was continuing:

Behind you your family will stay. I will give you the glories of the world! The gaiety of life will be yours and yours alone. No worries nor sadness! No more household chores. No more child rearing!

"Why would I leave my family?" I experienced a *strong feeling of wealth in money and all sorts of riches and successful businesses.* "I don't understand."

Then give me your hand and do my command—for 'tis on the highest land you stand.

This was said with a happy chuckle. I responded, "My family and I are one."

Not since this day began.

Again, I *felt* the experience of walking out on my

family—leaving and never looking back—and having a life of party time, millions of dollars, all sorts of successes and many admirers. I said, "But you said our—me and my husband's, love—is eternal and we will never separate."
That was before you reached the golden gate.
I thought, What's going on here? Who are you?
I am the prince of fate. Come.

This was said with great pride and expectancy. A command which was to be obeyed. It seemed I shouted—in my mind—not aloud. "No! Get behind me Satan! Be gone! I serve but one master, that of Jesus Christ sent by God in Heaven to save man from sin and to rise again and to leave with us the Holy Spirit. He alone do I recognize and He alone will I serve. Be gone!" I felt the currents of air surrounding me gather in a whirl and even *heard* a swish as the air went out through my front door.

I was in shock. I sat in stunned silence. How can mere words describe utter disbelief? Not a breath of air seemed to remain in my living room. The stillness was suffocating. I searched my mind for a wrong in my actions. How did I let myself be put into such a position as to be tempted by the Devil? I had thought Satan was a figment of someone's mind to threaten people into the correct actions in their lives. Guess I would have to re-think that! No way did I think this little Episode up! No way! There was a devil and he was active. Also, very attractive with his invitations. He carried with him the feel of fun, excitement and wealth. A carefreeness that I suspect all humans would envy. Yes, he would be difficult to turn down. I knew one thing. I'd never forget that he exists, regardless of the many ways I've heard him explained away—usually as a negative force or negative thinking. Huh uh.

I sat there frozen in space. My home had been invaded, and how had I known those words to say? I read the last paragraph I had written down. I could never have known those things to say. It had to have come from the source of the Holy Spirit, my protector, for I had not known how to write those words.

Yeah, this had been a scary experience. I was still feeling it.

The following afternoon I wrote: "Was Satan talking to me yesterday?"

Yes, he is evil, he is cunning. You did recognize him and send him on his way. This is necessity to know he is ever active. For some do not believe there is such. Some believe there are no other spirits than God—yet my works are done by many, my praises sung by many. It was important to be assured there is a devil, actively at work, and to be of assurance because another said, aloud, 'Look up and trust all to your father in heaven,' is needed to put man wise.

Now go forth in glory array to meet the dawn of a new day. Peace to you and yours.

"What do you mean by 'on highest ground'? Satan used it too, although I was sure for him it was a farce."

To be on a hillside is of great importance so your light can shine over the water yet a greater distance for all to see. To the east is the flawless sunrise to lift to the skies the spirits each dawning of all who look toward the east and to

God, for it is hereby that we look to God to magnify our every thought and our every action guided to be forever at His side. You we placed on higher ground for all to see the change.

Scary! That's enough for one day! My brain could take no more!

I was so confused! "I have lost track of who I am and what I am to do. Please, can you help me pray for answers, understanding and wisdom? But how do I pray?" Then, it seemed I knew these words to write:

> *Dear Jesus, I come to you on bended knee*
> *Asking, Who might I be?*
> *Where am I, here in this life,*
> *Struggling, battling strife,*
> *On my way to greater glory*
> *Or do I fold in this foray?*
> *I wait your answer of great insight*
> *To purge—gather strength in my plight*
> *Or wither, die, and not ask why.*
> *Answers you gather of great renown*
> *And seek again for which you're bound*
> *A child of God—though gingerly you trod*
> *Always waiting for my nod.*
> *Now go my child in line of duty*
> *To fulfill your goals to their annuity*
> *For here you find your greatest gifts*
> *One's clear of any rife*

Council of Angels

And thus from this day forward
Walk in faith; your trust in The Lord.
Now I know who I am and whence I came
Is not for me to apologize nor hang my head in shame
For God has given me all the tools I need
To daily grant another use of a kindly deed.
My home is open to passersby: A house of love
Actions to comply with guidance from above
To lift the aura into blue and pink
Can happen if you give life a wink.
And study, too, that which makes you think
So into doldrums you will not sink.
Fragrances and birds' songs will light the way
Changing a dank, dark hour into a bright, shiny day.
Grateful am I.

Jo Long

Pans & Things

For the next few days I steered clear of my living room and did not write. I kept busy doing household chores. Yet habit is strong and at 6:00 o'clock one morning I asked for answers.

"The pans aren't paid for yet. When. . ."

Soon. Tenfold and more will they be paid for.

"OK. Anything else?"

God's plan is beyond the understanding of mortal man. The soul has a knowledge of greatness far greater than the human eye can see. For man is a shell of mobile activity carrying the soul to fulfill the necessary duties to motivate God's plan. So as to take pride in beauty of a car is also taking pride in beauty of body. To foretell the grace of God is to accompany a feeling of duty. The responsibility comes in the relaying of the true meaning so it is not misconstrued.

"Our Slim needs a prayer, please."

Be where my daughters footprints trod. Lift her up from the depth of despair. Show her you are there. Make her way her own thus so much less to atone. Hold not her mistakes as yokes but let them be only strokes to wend her way day by day. Oh God, when she stumbles lift her gently; brush the cinders from her knee. Let her know we care, you and me. Ever in Your keeping.

"Thank you Lord. It seems to me we have so much difficulty living with our fellow man."

Yes. Well, you cannot be on earth and not be aware of the many conflicts to fellow travelers. Each in a different phase of learning. No—not age as you count it. For a child can perceive greater than the earthly father and a young woman can be amazed at the greater understanding of her small sister. So it can not be age as you count for the abundance stored. Well then it must come from the knowledge of the soul—usually untapped by man.

"Should we be using our soul knowledge?"

Would be of amazing aid to use it daily but only of great and unenduring times do we recall this supply of needs.

"Is there a way to use it in times other than stress?

By an abundance of faith will it be opened to you.

The following morning I wrote, "Do you have a message of learning?"

Go ye then to prepare a path for men. For they seek after the clatter of likeness in fellowman. By their tongues will ye know them and by this means show them the paths they tread lead to mire. To be of help to themselves they must turn about but because of their own desire. For it is here the difficulty does appear. Their ways of inequity are sweet until they become deep. The flesh is surface and no lasting ill but of depth does it reach the soul, and either it be good or bad but not a little of both for can a drink be both sweet and sour? No. For the taste then becomes bitter. So it is with souls—tainted is of impurity and only can life be come of a purity to be allowed to reach God.

"But we reach God on faith."

No, We receive freedom of our worldly sins. Still do we seek God. For he reigns on high and we grow by levels of His learning. Each step is upward. A step backward is a step lowered. We build our paths upward as stepping stones. Our salvation is beside God and our helping hand comes thru Jesus Christ as a personality and is accepted as the Holy Ghost for each of us he is available.

"Is it always so difficult to find and accept the aids of the Holy Ghost?"

Each in his own way and of great desire. It is that man is dependent upon his initiative but at a time of great turmoil does he then reach out to a greater aid.

"But some strive so hard to be Godly and still do not find the way."

Each in their own time.

That Friday evening I wrote: "I had a lovely day but am up tight here at home. Why?"

It is you expect too, too, too much for one day. Do not

be afraid of what your family says; they are only happy when you are happy; take time to be happy for them also.

"I feel guilty for not doing all I said I would do this day."

If you plan miles only plan one or two stops. Today you made how many? Also of that nature you can not accomplish so very much in one day and be of good cheer and find contentment in the day. Praise your daughter for her accomplishments. Today she fixed food for herself, father and boys, dressed boys, and took them to school. Made beds. P.M. helped with boys and supper and dishes. You expect much in one day. Listen more carefully to her daily adventures and go with her to the horse barn and pasture.

Do not argue with your husband nor try to prove—soon will be discarded this laxness of belief.

Do not plan so much for one day and the tension and stress will leave you relaxed and happily capable to care for family interests.

Wee one is anxious to use her ability to create her clothes. Put this in an available position and let her grow. You will enjoy it with her. All. Rest.

6:30 Saturday morning. "I am ready to receive."

Ahhhh the morning is fresh and crisp. A good hour to start your day. The dove promises eternal love. The rain crow his promise keeps.

"I heard the dove and the rain crow!"

Rain will be plentiful. Now, yes, the glories of God's treasures are free to all if they will only listen. To reap what you sow is a misconception. We reap—you sow. . .the sowing done by many. There are those who do not sow but reap. . . .But I say to you: Only the good sow the good and even so they have to sort at reaping time. Also does the father sow only the good yet the chaff is even sorted from the good before they enter into the kingdom of heaven. Now also is it the same in life. You sort as you go but yet again it is to separate chaff before the final storage. Remember, yet even the unforeseen can enter into a field and cause rot and mildew that no man can prevent. . .A beautiful field of flowing golden wheat—a beauty for every eye to behold—may produce only a sparse amount of grain to be used to the good of mankind. The rest is called by-products and is of small use for lower animals but small amount of value even then. Yet can a field of wheat heavy of grain be of more yield but not so much of the beauty is seen while in the field. Also rough grain is less attractive to all who behold it and is less apt to become so infected by passing evils. So is man—a beautiful man or woman is always made aware of that beauty. All others want to become a part of the beautiful one. But to become apart of must include also the touching of the other. The touching is a process of leaving stain on the beauty. For seldom is the beauty leaving anything on the tainted. . . .As a morning—untouched—but the day changes. . . .So God's world is a clean promise for man to take part of but never to be left tainted by the previous hours. A clean start. To keep it clean, mar it not.

When dreams are being fulfilled, and the reaping of life

Council of Angels

is thru God's abundance, only tranquillity reigns—not fatigue. Do not plan so many operations, for it is our work you'll be doing. Also, the bodies will be adequate. There will be space and time for all desires and no frustration or strain. For He is in charge of each life on this location and it is of no consequence to you and your's, the other ways of the world.

"I don't understand this last? Can you explain further?"

By way of living it will be made in a most unusual manner but so as to release all strain of worldly gain. Our work is of necessity. Manuscript is to be.

"Are you still telling me I am to be the author of a book?"

Yes. One that will open eyes more than any other on the bookshelves.

"You told me to 'compile' but I could compile for years and still not be able to write a book! Isn't it a waste of time to compile? My spelling is horrible! My typing isn't so hot either. What would I write? It seems to me it would be much better to choose a person who is already a writer. At least one who can spell."

A person who is already writing would not be molded to our ways so easily. You are of the right material for our purpose for many reasons. Your belief. Already you have the ability to reassure your fellow man.

It is not a necessity to spell but to hear and feel. . .is of great importance. Many are perfect on the type machine but too busy to listen. Your typing will improve. So many of man's activities are understood by you. Many soon forget past experiences. You can recapture them—feeling and actions.

Next to be reckoned with is ridicule. For there will be much. Do not become unreasonable. Now is coming soon the time to write. *Your compilings are for experience and reference for many others—not us. Also for yourself. As you see things unfold your writings can be seen where and when it was foretold.*

"Will you be my helper in this book?"

I will be here beside you—your constant guide, your companion for evermore. Yours to confer and talk to as now on any and all subjects, day or night. Many will be the personalities of the book. . . .There will be many books. Not one. For your task will become easier in receiving and putting down—and in understanding our conception of man's world

"What is the title of the first book—do you know?"

Yes. It is, 'God Is For All People.'

"How much longer before we are ready to start?"

We are ready. It is you we wait on.

"Oh! What is my next action?"

I had placed my antique typewriter on a card table in my living room several weeks ago. So now, I went to it and sat down, my fingers on the keys ready to write. But—what? As I contemplated, the voice spoke in my ear. I wrote: *This is a time of great unrest and lack of sufficient leadership. Man basically needs to follow, for God made him that way. He is not self-sufficient, as he would like to believe, and quickly forgets that he is completely dependent upon his maker, God, in Heaven and only thru Jesus Christ can man be heard by God. Only thru the great unbound abundance of our Gracious Heavenly Father has man the many luxuries he abounds in today. For it is only thru God's Grace that man has progressed. . .to manufacture these many comforts of our day. Since God is responsible for each hair on your head, is it not believable? He is also responsible for the food you eat, for the comforts, where you sleep and for the grain you reap? For too long has man been away from the teachings of the Bible and the search of his master and God. . . .*

God made the earth as we know it. He did make it for the man He put in it. The abundance of the food and fowl were plentiful. Never has God taken away such abundance. Never has He reproached man for his greediness, only has He shown great patience. Still man has not searched out the reasons for his abundance and for the true complete plan of God. So now is the time for such to take place. Do you realize that man is searching today for every avenue open to him to find the true and lasting meaning of the life, world, universe and God's plan for mere man?

I was amazed! I had typed this with out spelling one word wrong or making one typing error.

So, this was the way "I" was to write a book. I certainly didn't understand it but I could do it.

In the days that followed I set aside the first hour of my day to write. Some times I would be at it for twenty minutes. Some days longer or shorter but never over one hour. At times, when interrupted, I would stop typing in the middle of a sentence, paragraph or even a word. Yet, as I returned the next morning to resume the writing—without review—there was no break in the thought or wording. Then I would go to my pen and notebook and do my meditative time. This was a very determined routine to the end of the book. Amazement was continual. The end of the book arrived and again I was surprised as it was only a small number of pages. I had expected to be writing a huge book. One of many, many pages.

With the "hearing" and "writing" of the book came many questions. I had accepted the idea of spirits or entities as helpers. Some way I was receiving the words in my ear and I was asking how. One morning I asked, "I wonder, can you tell me about spirits?"

The spirit as a personality remains the same and is retained in the soul to be used at times of great need. Although the soul has a different shell or body it has retained all the memories of each personality and is stored as a learning process for future use. So can the soul be 'living' again as you would put it and yet a portion of the past as in a spirit form depart from and go to any needed place or person. Such as you know the greatness of a mother's love, to divide the love for another child does not lessen the abundance stored. So is the many spirits of the soul.

"What is a ghost?"

A ghost as you refer is truly an earth-bound spirit. For so many reasons are different spirits earth bound.

"What are some of them?"

Some spirits cause such havoc they lose their place in the growth of the chain of knowledge and have to remain in their last place of dwelling 'til such a time they have decided to repent their ungodly ways and seek righteous ways.

"Do people really see ghosts?"

Yes, at times. For it is a way of showing man is not in charge of all things.

"Can ghosts do bodily harm to people?"

At times. For this is usually a climax to great injurious wrongdoing in a previous journey. A spirit of great strength can remain on earth to correct a grievance at a costly price to the spirit.

"Why 'a costly price to the spirit'?"

Because to believe God is in control is a must. To take control is a mistake.

"If God is in control why does he let this happen?"

God is not in control unless one lets him be.

"Sometimes it seems the Godly people suffer much more than the ungodly. Can you explain?"

The Godly will still reap goodness in heaven.

"But it seems they reap only hardship on earth."

No—tranquillity comes even in worse poverty or in face of danger in a battlefield. This does not mean protection in earthly life. This can mean protection in the next life. This does not mean worldly wealth in the same life, but to follow life. They are accumulative.

"Then if a person on earth now is living an ungodly life but has acquired many worldly riches he is reaping worldly comforts from a previous life?"

No! He is living a learning process. Because they have riches does not mean a life of ease. They can be having all sorts of conflict inside and also outside. It is only a different station to be learned by each soul. So many are the spirits of wrong doing, they cry in the night and knock on the doors or hearts of men for their pity and condemnation. But they are to be rejected, for only one way can they achieve the kingdom of heaven, by paying for their sins to repenting.

"Is there a place they go to repent?"

Some call it purgatory.

"Do all souls have to go there before going on to their next life?"

Only those of great wrong doing.

"What is the difference in the good and bad spirits. How does one tell?"

Some are foreboding—not pleasant—nor desirable to be a comfort to. Some are. . .loving companions as a friend who never desire choices of dire straits.

"Now, this, I can relate to. But, are the good ones angels?"

There are many stations of angels. Many names of reference. Many duties to accomplish. The name of such is of small importance. The identity of relationships is the

Council of Angels

ultimate.

To accept the contact asked for is immanent. *As grows the acceptance, so grows knowledge. . .due to a man's abilities to accept a way foreign to worldly acclaim. Such as to share with another on life's plane is not the accepted act, but to grow in wisdom and knowledge, then is it to be accepted by fellow travelers—teachings referred to as help from angels, word from God or spirit, entity or guardian, —these are all words to describe heavenly or spiritual guidance.*

"I've had enough for one day. Thanks and bye now."

Jo Long

Helping Hands

The starting of another week. Art put my six heavy cases of merchandise in the car then he, Slim and the boys left for their day.

I checked the crock pot, tuned it from high to simmer, picked up my purse and headed for the door. "Wow!" I thought. "This is such a beautiful day. My first appointment is at 10:30 so I'll have an hour to spend with Sybil."

Sybil answered my knock with a smile and told me, "Ann is having trouble again. I just know it! I have been worryin' all night."

I sat at her table as she placed the steaming cup of coffee before me. What could I say? "Maybe you're suppose to pray?"

"I did that just before you came in. I only said, 'God, take care of my girl'. I didn't know what else to say."

"I think that should be enough. We can only put our loved ones in His hands." Then I added, "And trust it is so."

She placed a plate of cookies on the table next to her cup of coffee. I could see she was really upset and nervous.

This had been an on-going problem and Ann was afraid to leave her husband for fear of what he would do to her and the children. Her life was a living soap-opera—straight from the T. V.

Sybil and I talked of other things concerning the neighborhood.

"So, where are you off to today?"

"The beauty shop in Crestwood. An hours drive. We have an hour to visit before I need to hit the road. What are you doing?"

"Tracy asked me to watch her youngest today while she goes to the dentist."

"That'll keep you busy—and happy. She's a cutie. Are you ready for Bunco tonight?"

"Yeah and I have my gifts wrapped," she said as she picked up the coffee pot to refill our cups. On her way back to the counter she stopped in mid stride and turned to me with a surprised look on her face. At the same time I heard a little bell make a ding-a-ling sound. "Oh!" Sybil exclaimed. "I heard my little bell! I know Ann's all right. Did you hear it?"

"I heard a little bell. Where is it? It sounded sorta raspy."

"That's my little bell to let me know all is well. Oh! What a relief! I know Ann's not in danger."

I had never heard that bell before. Nor had I heard this idea before. Was Sybil losin' it?

I sat quietly a few seconds, listening, my eyes searching every nook and cranny, before I asked, "Where is that bell?"

"I don't have a bell. It's just the sound I hear."

"O.K. I heard it, too. Don't believe I can relate to this but if you say so, I believe it. I heard it clearly. It sounded raspy to me but it definitely was a little bell."

"I call them my little silver bells. They sound as if they're in a deep well, don't they? This started when I was worried about Nick last week. He's only sixteen and is doing a man's work evenings after school. For some reason I really got upset about him and then I heard the little bell and knew he was in no danger. It's a wonderful relief. Just another fabulous experience we share. Some would think us balmy, but the feelings so exhilarating! It makes the rest of my day or night. I can sleep like a baby after hearin' it. It's a miracle."

I got up and prepared to leave. "My hour's up. I have to go now but this has certainly been a great way to start our day. See ya tomorrow, I think."

I was about twenty miles further down the road when I could stand it no longer. I pulled my car to the shoulder and wrote:

"Can you tell me—is it O.K. for me to ask about the bells? What are they?"

The time bells are silver. They are minute—extremely small. A way of preparing a person for our presence. You thought it was the telephone, doorbell and the stove timer. This is letting you know we are near and you can hear. In this case, to let Sybil know her daughter was in our care.

"Thank you."

Council of Angels

Thank you was all I could say. I was stunned! I felt about two inches tall. Boy! No little silver bells for me. I had to have the door bell, telephone and stove timer. Even when my stove had no timer on it! But that stove timer had been loud enough to wake me from a deep sleep! And the time my house was full of company and I heard the telephone ring. I got so upset because no one answered— Oh Boy! No wonder I got those odd looks. It was taking me a while to digest this. As I recalled those days I actually felt embarrassed. I remembered all right. It all started one Sunday when relatives from a distance came for a special dinner and to spend the evening. Twenty-five, in all. our house was full to the brim. I loved having them.

While I was busy getting the dinner together, I heard the door bell. No one else seemed to hear it. I supposed it was because they were talking so loud. I became rather frustrated with the lot of them. In a huff, I made my way through the crowded dinning room, toward the living room and to the front door, scolding them on my way by making the remark, "Can't any of you people find time to answer the doorbell?"

The room became very quiet. I reached the front door and jerked it open. No one was there. Going back through the dinning room I remarked, "They're gone. No one was there." The remark was received in complete silence, with questioning looks shot in my direction.

It was in the afternoon, with dishes nearly finished, I heard the telephone ring. No one answered it. Glancing into the dinning room, I saw Harvey sitting beside the telephone. I said, "Harvey, will you please answer the phone?"

He looked perplexed, but made no move to pick up the receiver. Again, the room became very quiet.

Almost immediately I heard the telephone ring again. This time, I simply walked into the dinning room full of people and answered it. No one was on the line. "I sure hope they're happy. Couldn't even wait a few seconds before they hung up. Maybe they'll call back."

No response. Conversation came to a halt. The quietness caused me to realize I was not acting the part of a gracious hostess. What was my problem?

I didn't have time to dwell on the telephone episode. I had things to do: dishes to put away, children to check on, and I was getting tired. I was getting irritable. Short on speech and long on frustration. I kept busy.

Our company stayed through the supper hour and left shortly before bed time. This left me with the extra food to pack into smaller containers, good china and silver to store, the long tablecloth to wash, and, with help from Art, three extra leaves to remove, to reduce the long table to the small, daily size. I put on a clean tablecloth and got the boys into the tub for their bath. Slim had been my full-time baby sitter for the long day and she surely was weary of the care the boys demanded.

Bedtime came late. I was exhausted.

Chigger was still 'on the go'. I lay in my bed listening to his restlessness. The poor little guy could not fall asleep.

I dragged myself out of bed, went in to him and started

to rub his back. He flipped over and put his soft, chubby arms around my neck and gave me a kiss, then wrapped his legs around my waist, wanting to go rock in the big chair. So, our night routine began—again.

At 2:15, when I crawled into my bed, every bone and muscle in my body ached. Surely Chigger would sleep a little later the next morning.

Nope! At 5:30 a.m. I heard those little feet hit the floor. I pretended to be asleep as I heard him head for the kitchen in a dead run. But when I heard the clink of the sugar-bowl lid, I could pretend no longer.

One arm in the sleeve of my robe and struggling to find the other, I rounded the corner to the kitchen, to be greeted by the picture of Chigger on his hands and knees, his little bare butt dimplin' at me as he strained to reach another spoon full of sugar from the bowl in the middle of the table. How did he manage to get his diaper off? On hearing me, he spilled the heaping spoon of sugar and turned to give me his most winning smile. Why fight it? Just give him a hug, get him fed, and into the toys.

At breakfast Art asked me, "What was it that made you think the door bell rang yesterday?"

"Because it did." I snapped.

"You're the only one who heard it."

"I suppose that was because you were talking too loud."

"It didn't ring. The telephone didn't ring either. Harvey was sitting right beside it."

"How do I know. I heard it clear as a bell. I can't know everything. Big deal!"

By the time my family were off to school and delivered to the babysitter I was ready to go back to bed. I telephoned Sybil.

"Sybil, yesterday was a big Sunday dinner and a late night. Do you mind if we skip our reading this morning?"

"No, this is a blue Monday for me and I'm movin' slow. Maybe a little later."

"Great. I'm going back to bed. I'll see ya."

No bed ever felt better! The covers were soft and warm, the house was quiet and each of my family were in a safe place. All I had to do was sleep.

I was awakened by the "ding" of a timer. Irritated, I threw the covers off of me and went in to the kitchen to push the alarm off before it could ding again.

I stood in front of the stove, looking at it. "Now this is dumb!" I said out loud. "This stove doesn't have a timer on it. What did I hear?"

I went back to bed; laid there for a while, thinking on the stove timer. I couldn't understand it. Then I looked at the clock. It was 2:30 p.m.! I had slept the day away! My family would be home in one hour. I hurried out of bed, got dressed and started my days chores. No need to consider any sales for this day. I could get supper started and a cake in the oven; roll out some pie crust for cinnamon swirls, so the kids would have a quick snack; have the house neat, beds made, and a load of wash in. Heck! I'll even have a cup of coffee ready to share with Art. Not much time for the two of us to be together these days.

Golly! Those early days with the boys were truly

traumatic. Somewhere in there we were becoming a happy family and were having good times together. Our lives were beginning to level out to a workable, enjoyable experience. Surely families were to be happy, not in constant turmoil and bickering.

I sat down for a few minutes to write. I asked, "Is Ann a fool for staying with her husband when he is so mean to her and the children?"

You mean should she be putting faith and trust in this person. As you search for true love ask these questions.

Is he worthy of trust and affection—for here are the most treasured of all treasures.

Is he stable—a dependable nature? To trust him is to also then trust herself.

Does he care for her and the child as if they are his best arm, his best eye and his only life.

To find a companion who will fill hours of loneliness by happy and contented thoughts is a must. A life of frustration is as a boat with a broken oar. God made man superior of his animal world because of the ability to choose his road in life. She should know her freedom to make her own choice; not another's choice for her life. She should fear not the difficult path and then choose the lesser of the two routes. Set morals as follows.

Be ye of possession of body and soul, for unless you welcome with pleading and open arms none can enter

Take charge of your life

Alone you are lost, turn then to your God in heaven He waits your beckoning call.

"But *how* can we tell others—even our dearly beloved children—these things?"

Prayer of earnestness is the trail to the plea of rigorous intent as water is on a tightly strung tent. To force the thought is to nag and can only be heard as the chatter of geese.

"Thank you and Praise the Lord! We people lack so very much in knowing what to do. I will pass this information on to Sybil tomorrow. Now, for my sales."

Council of Angels

Wrenching Days

Life has a funny way of holding you human. All of this spiritual learning to believe matters of earth are secondary and then to find yourself in a 'pickle o' fish' you had nothing to do with! Now comes the turmoils, pain and frustrations of complexities of very human mankind. And, takes the form of very human actions.

The court was taking the boys back. After a year of our best care, food, teaching and coping. According to our very man-kind laws, we could do nothing about it. We had no right, opinions or feelings. We could be used whenever possible and dumped at leisure. No word of appreciation or even acknowledgment of having given time and love, energy and anguish. As if it had never been. To visit was never an issue. It wouldn't be possible. Our only hope was to hope when they were older, and when on their own, they would want to visit us. Again, I turned to my writing.

"Our hearts are heavy and we are perplexed."

Keep the faith and trust the Lord to do the rest. Let not yourself submit to fear but move in an assured way. Not

Jo Long

one of defeat. Let supremacy reign. Put on your armor and look up for guidance. Let your guidance come from us—through trust and faith.

It was hard to remember to look up. That meant inside a building or outside, looking up to receive prompt contact with the universal powers.

"What can we do?"

Pray for the mother.

What do you mean—pray for the Mother? After all the trouble she has been? How can I do that when you told me one has to love another to pray for them?

To put all else from your heart and earnestly pray to God for one's deliverance is a way of faith and of utter forgiveness and is giving her the greatest gift of all gifts. Don't you want this if it means a home and mother for your two precious charges?

"I want them to have a home and good care! Doubt if that drip can give it to them. I want them taken care of."

Then pray.

"I don't feel love for the mother, even though I know she *is* the mother. I don't believe this is in the best interest of the boys. It is only another way to hurt and cause trouble. She doesn't really want to take care of them."

Think only of the benefit to the young ones who need a young mother and a home. Ask the Father in heaven to coat you with the added love needed to pray for the mother and give her the eternal gift.

"I suppose I can do that if He helps me. Nothing else to do anyway. What do I say?"

Council of Angels

Our God in heaven, deliver for us this lost and seeking soul. For her's is the way of destruction. Turn her about in her path and show her the true meaning of life as a giving, caring, devoted mother. Lift her up, give her caring of others whom she can reach not. Give her a feeling of oneness and contentment. Put in her heart a way of understanding of others. Unbind her guilt and shower upon her true love of greatness. . . .For her to know love is to first feel love. Let your radiance shine as a vibrant heat. Beat all else in her heart to retreat. Cleave her only to her mate and thru him relate the change so he, too, his way will forsake. Make her awake and aware for his sake, we ask it. Amen, amen and amen.

Now put only faith to work, for hear this. Fear not— your vigil no longer keep, the children are as safe as in their sleep in God's care you had a share. Alas.

"Alas?"

Putting to work another way 'alas' can also mean 'farewell of sweet ways, for enjoyment was here many days'.

This did not mean we had no more hard feelings toward the mother, the stupid judge and our crazy civil laws—nor that I felt any better about them. My understanding was not a whit broader. Yet, when I wrote, I did have a feeling of 'letting go' and could then pass this feeling on to Slim and Art. The house seemed empty and the toys lay is disuse. We felt a betrayal and deep loss. Slim's bedroom would be restored to accommodate only her, but still it would be empty. So would our house. The kittens felt dejected as they entertained themselves. At bed time I wrote again. I needed something.

"Dear God your presence is so great, beautiful and wonderful! To know you is to live. To feel your presence is a joy untold. Your strength and love are endless. How thankful I am for you, to be allowed to know you. My heart is bursting in gratitude, my eyes brimming with tears of overwhelming. How I thank you."

Now go—your way will be lit. Sing your joys and show in your countenance the things felt in the heart.

I certainly had not expected to receive anything like this! The first was praise, the second part told me what to do. But again I asked, "Is she (meaning their mother) of Satan?"

No, not of Satan just a predicament of mans' making. Have you not seen children grow as flowers of beauty from the center of a trash dump. The flower is yet of greater beauty due to the poorness of location and surroundings.

Another day

"Snow has fallen during the night. Our lives are changing due to the boys leaving. Our day lies ahead. Can you be of assistance in charting it?"

A way of enjoyment is to turn again to simple uncomplicating tasks of the house. Be prepared for next phase of life's cycle in attempting again the completion of pre-planned goals. Put forth extra effort and much determination in this area for herein lies the foundation for

Council of Angels

all. Be staunch in faith our Lord embrace as herein lies His grace. Peace. Bliss.

Art came in. "I'm going to take their clothes and toys in to the boys. Do you want to come with me?"

"I don't think I can be civil. Are you sure you can?"

"There's no need to think of them coming back. It's the way of our times. They need clothing and their toys here remind us of them. Might as well make a clean break of it. If we are considerate, maybe they will be reasonable. I can see what kind of an environment they're in."

"I'll get their things ready for you, but I think I had better stay here. You sound as if you have a good attitude. I don't!"

"Where's Slim? Do you think she would want to go and see the boys?" Art asked.

Slim didn't want to go and Art made the trip alone. He was back within the hour, reporting a clean and seemingly happy family. Boy, does that help!

At bed time Slim called the kittens to put them in the basement which had been the routine since they first came. They were not to be found. Art took the flashlight and he went with Slim to search—but no kittens were found. Nor did they appear the next day.

A week later, when I unlocked the back door the first thing in the morning, I saw something flat and furry lying on the ground. It was not the carcass—only the golden yellow fur. I knew it was 'Goldie' and I also knew the kittens were gone as surely as the boys were. This was not surprising as we had nearly given them up, but the other idea that came to mind was surprising:

Hebrews 13:2. Don't forget to be kind to strangers for some who have done this have entertained angels unaware.

Could this be? Those babysittin' kittens had certainly changed lives. Now they had disappeared as mysteriously as they had appeared. Confused, I simply said, "thank you Lord, your many mysterious ways."

Council of Angels

Holding On

I was still having difficulty getting my life back on track without the boys. It was silly and I knew it was silly. Never the less, I was in a dunky mood—feeling empty, defeated and down on the world. The supply of groceries was low and I was not in the mood to go out and make extra money. I was ready to quit my direct-sales business. I didn't want to see anyone. I had no ambition to make contacts so I could sell my product. This was called depression. Finally, I made myself write. I hadn't in several days.

"I'm perplexed and feel so helpless! Can you help me?"

Many are. Sing songs of praise to Jesus and salute His deeds of grace from God. Shower on fellow man gifts of love in presence and thoughtfulness.

"I need to go buy groceries. I just feel so all alone and perplexed. Will you help me get my groceries? Now that sounds silly! Sorry. Just in a dither."

I am at your command to assist where you do not

understand. Be of peace of mind in way of desire do our lives entwine.

"I've done nothing today I planned to do. Just wasted the day away! Seems I've no ambition. I'm too tired and worn out to even think. Gonna go get groceries, stop for a Pepsi in a restaurant."

I tell you—dispose of many of your accumulations—keep only that which you need. Do not despair so!

"How can I help it? We never get to replace *anything* we get rid of. You say it will be different—but our bills are great and we need to pay Pearl for the pans. Yes, I feel despairing. I see nothing gained. I feel so helpless. We really need help. Can you help us?"

You know I can.

"Well, will you or not?"

In time comes all things. Put faith to work for here is action in commitment and desire. Go. . .leave the delivery to higher powers. Rejoice. Sing and praise God for his gifts thru His Son of man, Jesus Christ.

With a little disgust and much perplexity I made myself get to the grocery store. I could say I felt a little better as I drove into the city, but in the back of my mind I think I was actually refusing to let go of my drab feeling. Now, this was a new thought. No one in their right mind would want to hang on to the feelings I was having. And I could, in no way, Sing! On the return home, I turned on the car radio.

Council of Angels

Art was out of bed and starting his plans for the day. The telephone rang. It was one of my customers. She had three or four of her friends who wanted my product. I told her I would be over by 1:00 p.m. I would drop him off at the house where he was working and then keep my appointment. He was tearing down a three-story house for the lumber

Really, the day was a beauty. Crisp, cool enough for work outdoors. The kind of a day Art enjoyed. As we drove through the country I decided to see what he thought about me giving up my direct sales work.

"Art, I'm sick of this struggle to make money selling. How about me getting a full time job of some sort?"

"I think you've enjoyed your sales work in the past. Maybe you only need to give it some time."

"I'm sick of pushing sales and people.

"Any job will have people."

"I'm just tired. Tired of tryin'. Tired of keepin' appointments and sick of the world."

He put his arm around my shoulders and said, "I know. If you want to quit, it'll be all right." With that he got out of the car and then turned and said through the open window, "I'm sure those boys'll not come to any great harm and you did raise your family. They'll adjust and be happy with their mother. Stop your frettin'. We did our best and now it's time to move on to the next part of our lives. Whatever you decide is fine."

I put the car into gear and slowly drove on down the road to Katy's house—slowly, because the tears were foggin' my sight. How lucky I was to have Art. Darn it, I had a lot of money invested and if I quit, there was no way to get the money out of the merchandise. I had to dry my eyes before I reached Katy's. I parked, blew my nose and dabbed my eyes. Then I took deep breaths until I could calm myself.

Katy had four other women around the kitchen table having coffee. A fire was blazing in the family room which was a continuous part of the kitchen. Their warm smiles and glad greetings matched the bright-colored clothing they were wearing and the Christmas music on the hi-fi. All of this made me feel better. They really appreciated my coming. Wonder why that was a surprise. She had asked me to come.

When I left there an hour and a half later I had delivered the merchandise from my present stock and had appointments for the following week. I had collected $270.00. Katy wanted me to return the following day as some of the people she had invited couldn't be there.

When I got back to where Art was working, I was elated about the amount of money I had collected so easily. He came to the car and I showed him the money.

"Huh! I don't know what other type of a job you could collect that much money in one and a half hours."

"Yeah. There's no way I can quit this. We can't afford to. Besides I have to go back there tomorrow because she had some women who couldn't make it today. I told her I'd be back. Do you want to work here again tomorrow?"

"Depends on the weather.

Council of Angels

That night after supper one of Art's hunting buddies came by. He had finally found a place to sell their winter's catch of coon hides that would pay a good price.

When Art came home he had $356.00!

This really took the financial pressure off of us and I was still going to Katy's the next day. I actually felt as if we were finally in gear. We had the money to pay one of the smaller bills. Now, I could concentrate on the next one.

At 3:am I was wide awake! What was it? Something had caused me to wake up. I was alert—as if I'd already had two cups of coffee. "What's going on?" I thought.

I took my book and pen into the living room to my favorite chair, and wrote: "Is there a reason I'm awake?"

To arise at a beautiful hour is any early hour. To be willing when the body longs to resist. To be able to feel exuberant is such a luxury. To be of such ideal of self is to be exceedingly content of spirit. For contentment of body is not to be expected. Only demanding. Final.

To be of such ideal of self—I was pleased with myself? Now this was a shock! I had the gall to think all the money we were taking in was a reaction to our actions! Ha! Then I heard more words and wrote:

Of all needs am I come. Be ye great in faith for herein lies the depth of trust. . .Be it ever so. Yet do I fail in deliverance of a great message to many. Follow my way of action and confirm my message by acceptance and understanding. Be ye a way and a light I seek and in me your reverence keep. To be of assistance is all I seek for through the love and trust of Jesus come all things. So, say,

In God I trust to deliver what is a must.

"Do you mean that you fail in deliverance of a great message?"

Yes, I too fail in many ways. Do you think I am perfection dealing perfection. He alone can be perfection. I am ever striving too, my work to do. In you can I be more active and through you deliver many messages that can otherwise go unheard. Yes, be my light, to show them the way is only through Christ—and here lies the way to all things.

This seemed too easy.

Seems to be simple—the life now. No? This is. People complicate their own lives yet most know not to look up for deliverance. Be of a measure. The guide and the life of deliverance is yours.

"A measure of the guide?"

Because the completeness is not wholly of you but through you.

"I'm sure of that. There's something I've been wanting to ask you but can't think of it now. Do you have anything of learning?"

The question was what about the ways of those who seek after freedom of ancestors? It is a way of complaint as of a spoiled child. Question: What of the ways of those who seek after the pursuit of joyous ways alone? They seek only the chaff and this they reap. Do you not know the emptiness of a morn, following an evening of gaiety and reckless ways of expression? Do not sow the emptiness of no concern if the reaping is to have fruits. The question of

Council of Angels

how a body responds to the sameness of concern is as predictable as the wind for the ways are many. Put away idle chatter and find fulfillment in guiding to deeper understanding. The seekers of depth are more than you think. The ways of guiding them also are more than you think. In attitude or happiness and acceptance of the darker weather. For need is of both.

"Thank you. To think all of this started because I wanted money for bills. Well, now I have the money to pay all my bills and some over. How can I ever thank you?"

Say 'Praise the Lord' and bask in his bounties.

Jo Long

Looking Up

Friday morning came and Art was making a trip to the bank. I had prepared my order to send to the company for products needed to supply my customers.

"Since you're going to the bank, will you get a money order for the company for me?"

"I suppose so, although I prefer not to. Do you want me to drop it in the mail?"

"Yes, I'd appreciate it. I can get work done here while you're gone. Only—ask the amount of the money in my account and if it's not enough to cover the order you'll have to bring it back to me and I'll re-make it. I'm usually shorter in the bank than my check book shows. I think I have left enough, but you know how I make money errors. O.K.?"

"O.K." He was off and I quickly started the dishes and housework.

When I saw him walking up the side walk in our back yard I could see he was disgusted with me. "Darn," I thought. "I'm short money for that order."

Council of Angels

"You made me look like a fool! Don't ever ask me to do your business again."

"I told you I may not have enough money in the account to fill that order. What was so bad about that? I'm sure this isn't the first time that's happened."

"It wasn't *short*. You have over $500.00 in that account. You've been holding out on me."

"But the order was for over $400.00, so that's not too bad."

"*After* the order! You have over $500.00! I want to know where it came from."

I was speechless. No way could that be possible. Short, I could understand, as I was more often than not, but to have over $500.00! No way. I'd just have to go check it out myself.

Art went out to his shop. I sure wasn't going to argue with him until I found out what the bank had to say. Besides, it was sort of funny. He was mad because I had too much money. Now that was a first!

I went to all the trouble of getting dressed, putting my makeup on and curling my hair. Going to the bank was not one of my pleasant tasks, so I wanted to look as presentable as possible.

I went to Pam's window. She often was the one I worked through. I simply said, "Pan, I seem to have a little problem. My bank book shows me having $29.89 after my order this morning. Will you check it for me?"

"Sure. I'll get your sheet." In a few seconds she returned. I looked at the page and there it was! Over

Jo Long

$500.00, just as Art had told me. I asked her, "Do you think this could be a mistake? I can hardly believe I have more in the bank than I thought."

"This shows your transactions back several months. I don't see how it could be an error. I'll run up your deposits and check it for you."

When she returned to me she said, "No, I see no error. You must've failed to enter a deposit. I have a list of deposits we gave you credit for. Maybe you can check them with your check book."

"O.K., and thank you."

When Art came in I was still going back over my figures. I found nothing—anywhere, that could possible account for that extra money. I told him as much and he said, "Here, let me check."

After some time he had to give up. He found no error. Perplexing! Anyway, I had enough to finally pay Pearl for those pans I'd given her a bad check for months ago. I said, "According to the bank I have enough in this account to pay Pearl for the pans. Shall I pay her?"

"Quick! Before it evaporates."

I had to giggle. Couldn't resist sharing this thought with Art. I said, "Bet this is the first time you were mad at me because I had too much money in the bank."

"Uh Huh. You aren't out of the woods yet. Let's see how long it takes the bank to catch up with you." But he did have a hint of a smile lingering on his face.

I telephoned Pearl. "Hey, do you still have that bad check I gave you for those pans?"

"Sure do."

"Can you meet me at the half-way point cafe about 1:30 today?"

"Oh, hey! Ya got money for me?"

"Yep, I do."

"1:30 it is. See ya."

By the time I arrived at the cafe, I had gone over, in my mind, every sale I had made from the beginning of the year. I had not made that many sales because I hadn't been working most of that time. I settled myself in a booth near a window and as I was waiting for Pearl I went over my check book one more time. I was still checking my figures when she arrived.

"Hey," she greeted me. "Did you win the lottery?"

"Not hardly." Was my reply. "Fact is, I've no idea what I've done. The bank says I have more money than my check book shows. Now how's *that* for good banking?" We both giggled. The idea was preposterous.

"Well, what're you doing there? Going over your figures or theirs?"

"Both. The bank checked. Art checked. And I've gone over and over these figures. I can't see how in the world this could be."

"Here. Let the ol' pro check it out. Must be some transposed figures 'er sumptin'," as she reached for my book and the bank papers.

After several minutes and two more cups of coffee she finally gave up with, "You know, I believe there is more than meets the eye here. How do you account for it?"

"I don't! Art says pay you quick. Do you have the old check I wrote you? Give it to me and I'll give you a fresh one.

From her billfold she took the worn check and I tore it up and gave her an updated one. "There. You can cash that and it won't bounce, if you hurry."

"Have you been doing your writing any more?"

"Yeah, and I don't understand it, nor can I explain it, but I'm sure this money did not come to me via my own means. However, Art has sold his coon hides and I've been having good luck with my sales and—Thank Goodness, I'm actually feeling ready to start living again. It wasn't easy to lose the boys."

"That's been a traumatic experience from the very start. Have you thought—the main reason you ended up with them, in the first place, was because they needed to know there was a kind of love like you and Art and Slim could give them? I've thought about it several times. In the first place, not many people could take two youngun's like them into their home and raise them as if they were their own. They must've needed something only you could give."

"I've never thought of it like that. At the time, it just seemed the only thing to do. Like buying those pans. Now they're paid for. Cash that check quick.

"Well, on a lighter note, did you play the lottery this week? We've been playing it and so far only lost a few dollars."

"No, I haven't gotten into it. Keep forgetting. I think I will when I go to the grocery store but it slips my mind.

"Well, why don't you ask, and see what *they* have to say about it."

Of course this was the usual thing anymore, when we got together, to write. I took out my book (which I carried with me) and asked: "We would like to ask you about playing the lottery. Should we buy tickets?"

For some yes, for you it is unnecessary, but not wrong. For here, again, is a higher control.

Pearl formed another question: "What is it that makes so many church people against gambling or games of chance?"

Because of the deeper involvement. . . .

"Then is this true of other forms of chance or gambling?"

Be it true in other things as hoarding, cards, drinking, eating, dancing, working, giving and taking. Man is made to find his own amounts of each. A point of too much is in each. If a feeling of wrongdoing persists—back off—everyone has this—for some a wrongdoing is one thing—for some another.

"I thought the same rule applied to all." I wrote.

Like the Ten Commandants. Yes, but this is in overindulgence.

"But so many religious people say the bible says *no* gambling and games of chance."

The Bible is a good and honest guide, but it is believed in many different ways.

"You say it is unnecessary for me, but wouldn't this be a way of securing money enough to pay our bills?"

For payment of bills—look up. They will be delivered. For those without this knowledge, it is a way. You are beyond this way and will want not. Nor your family want not. You will only prosper in fruits reaped.

"Can you show us how to pray for our needs?"

'*Our Father, look on us and our daily needs. Lessen the pains of remorse for the children and loved ones. Be ever present in their lives that they shell find their ways. Close not the hearts, but open them for praise. Be ye their comforter and protector all their days. Amen. For as ye seek so shell ye reap—and in finding a path, show it on to the next so their burdens can be lessened. This in His name. Amen, Amen and Amen.' Now rest in Peace for the ways of God are many.*

As always, this left us with new thoughts. We had to do some changing in our thinking, again.

Pearl remarked, "If this is a new way of living, we should enjoy it. For you to be long instead of short, in the bank, has Gotta be a new way of living'. Don't knock it. But, then, what can we say?" She giggled.

"Praise The Lord."

On my way home I was deep in thought. If this was the way man was *supposed* to live, he sure had missed it since the beginning of time. Then into my mind flashed the bible story about the woman who gave of her last bit of oil and flour—there after her larder never ran dry. Well! How could this apply to me? Yes, I (we) had given our best.

Could this mean our "supply" would never run dry?

This seemed a little much. But who was I to question the mysterious ways of God. With a deep sigh of satisfaction and serenity I drove home.

Jo Long

Hard Work Pays Off

Pearl had received a "lead" from her niece, Nellie. We were in the direct-sales business and when someone was interested in entering the business we were to contact them and train them. This particular woman lived in a distant state. We decided it would be the change we had been needing. Our families agreed and we made plans to make the trip.

Two days later we arrived at the woman's house while she was still at work. She had left instructions for us to make ourselves at home until she arrived from her 8: to 5: job, explaining that she usually had to work over and to not expect her before 6:00.

The house was neat. We brought in our suitcases and Pearl was finding the fixin's for coffee. I put the cups on the table from the cupboard and sat down to wait for Pearl to join me. Absent mindedly, I picked up a piece of paper pushed to the far side of the table and the pencil beside it. Immediately, I felt a quick catch of breath, as if I were in a rush, and then noticed the writing. It was a grocery list. A menu planned for the week's meals. I turned it over. Here was a list of to-do's she had marked off as they were done. Beside the many things listed were little square boxes of all shapes and sizes. Some had been traced many times.

My feelings of rushing were very strong. Then the doubts and fears of living! My mind felt cluttered with the things children needed and the hollowness of a lack of a husband. This was perplexing. I had never experienced anything like it before. "Pearl, I thought you said this woman was married."

"Yeah, and has four children. Ages 9 to 16. Why?"

"Well, I picked up this piece of paper and she has listed her groceries for the week and the things to do to get ready for our visit. She feels all boxed in and is very anxious about her children's activities. She feels deserted by her husband and he doesn't live here."

"Where did ya get all of that?"

"I don't know. Just came to me, as I was looking at her writing, here—on this paper."

"Let me see that." She took the paper and looked at it closely. "I only see she's a neat writer. Doesn't tell me anything else."

"She's a neat writer, and dresser and housekeeper. She's also very accurate in her office work. She works with figures—like in a bank or some such—and has her own way of doing things. She's a very nervous person and needs only 2 to 4 hours sleep at night. Golly! She should do great in this business. She could have a showing three or four times a week, she has so much energy. She needs money, too. But what's new about that?"

"This is crazy! What else can you find out about her? What about her kids?" Pearl was looking at me sorta funny.

"Well, her youngest is her dearest, right now. He's like a post she's leaning on. The others are being a pain in the butt. One is athletic—a boy. The oldest is a girl and she's worrisome about who the girl's running around with and dating. The other girl's a little pistol. She likes to stir things up so she can get personal points from her mother for being helpful. Ha! Some help she is. Stretches the truth a bit so things will be a little more interesting. She is, really, a precious little gal and will be a different person in a few more years."

"My Gosh! You're telling us their family problems. Here, let me write something. I want to know what you see for me." She reached for another piece of paper.

I was dumfounded. "Don't be silly. I know you."

"Well, I don't know what I will be like in a few more years."

"That's not important. I guess we need to know about these people. You know, we thought we were comin' out here to enroll her in the business, and maybe we are. But, we've really come to be of help to them as a family and in searching their way in life. You know what I mean? I mean this is due to the 'writings' as much, if not more, than the business."

"You're right. And we thought it was to help our business! Well, how little we know, huh?"

We each sat there several minutes with no words

passing between us. Pearl poured the coffee and we had the rolls we had brought with us.

"How are you gonna' help 'em?" Pearl voiced the same question I was asking myself.

"I don't know. I never thought I could help any one. These are complete strangers to me. I guess it's you who will help them."

"I didn't analyze her handwriting. I can't imagine how I could solve their problems."

"Well, guess we'll have to play it by ear. We must be here for some reason or I would not have gotten all the information from that grocery list. Then, too, we don't know if it's all correct."

"Oh yes we do. You know it and so do I. It'll be fun to find out from them how much truth there is in it. How will we find out? I've a feeling none of them are going to come in here and blurt out 'I got a problem,' you know. We'll have to feel our way along."

"I was told, wait until the door is opened, and then I would know what to say and how to say it. I've often thought it would be a good way to get a black eye."

We giggled at this, but neither of us felt like it was a laughing matter.

I mused, "How did I ever get to doin' this? Why me and not you?"

"Well, I'd say it was another development. You have been more persistent than I have with your daily contacts."

Kile was the first to come home from school. He came in the back door and gave us a slow smile, saying, "Hello.

We answered, "Hi." He went upstairs and was gone for some time.

When he came back, he had changed from school clothes to old jeans and went to the refrigerator to select something he put in the micro wave. Then he poured a huge glass of milk and got cookies from a jar. He ate in silence.

After some time Pearl said, "You must be Kile. I'm Pearl and this is my friend Jill." He smiled and said, "I know." He Continued eating.

When he finished his food, he put the used silver in the sink, replaced everything else to its proper place and said with a sigh, "I've gotta fix the chain on my bike before I can deliver my papers. Wish I had someone to hold for me. It would be easier. Rand doesn't get home 'til after the basketball game tonight."

"Oh Yeah? I helped my boys with their bikes. Bet I can hold for you. How 'bout it, will I do?" Pearl offered

"Sure. Come on."

Looking above his head we exchanged knowing glances. Here was a way of helping already and *we* had been asked.

Soon the bike was fixed and Kile was off to make his route. When Pearl came in she washed her hands and commented, "We didn't even have to make the attempt to help. That door was opened for us. How 'bout that for service."

"Yeah, and such a simple way to help, and it's caused you to be closer to that little boy already."

"Yeah, and we had quite a conversation, too. He said he had always needed help but his Dad was never around and his mother had to work to pay the bills and he had to do for himself. Then he added, 'But I know I have extra help because when I'm stuck on something the ideas just seem to come into my head.'"

"No!"

"Yep, that's exactly what he said. Seemed a simple solution to him, and no mystery about it."

"Ha! And no mystery about it! Oh Boy! From the mouth of babes, the simplicity of life."

Nellie came home early and in the course of getting acquainted we found the three of us were very congenial.

She was a petite woman in her mid 40's with dark, natural-wavy hair; quick, bright blue eyes and was not able to sit still a minute. She busied herself getting our supper on the table as we talked.

"Where do you work and what do you do?" I was curious.

"I'm a bookkeeper for the largest irrigation system in the state. I set up their books and keep them up to date. I have my own system of accounting and have introduced it to several other companies around here. This is a small town, but we have a lot of industry. Some of the larger companies settle here because of lower rents and taxes etc. I have a small group of accountants I'm teaching my system to. It's fun and I like it, but I can also do something else. My evenings are long and usually the only one home is Kile. He goes to bed early and I have the evening alone. The lady next door said she would come over and stay with him while I'm out selling this new product. Do you think it will work here?"

"I should think so. You find a starting point with someone interested to try it for herself. Do you have any one in mind?"

"I have three parties lined up for this week while you're here so you can get me started. Then from those, I'll have more bookings."

"Sounds like you've started the ball rolling. We'll spend our time in training you in every way we can think of. Ask us questions—any you can think of—and we'll try to answer."

"I have a lot of questions I wish someone could answer for me. They sure don't pertain to business, though. I can handle those. It's this confounded every-day life that gets me so bogged down. Rand thinks I should go to all of his games and Kile feels neglected. Debby and Gray are always fighting, and my damn husband is always giving me troubles. He thinks he can be gone for a month at a time and come back here to give us orders and hop in bed with me, get his jollies and be off again to some place I don't know where, and with someone I don't know who, then come back here and do it all over again the next month or even two months later. I'm sick of it and it will be changed. Oh!" She stopped short between the sink and the table. "I didn't mean to tell you all my troubles. That just slipped out. Here, let's eat. Food always helps." She had embarrassed herself and was trying to cover over. That was impossible, of course.

Toward the end of the meal and during a pause, Pearl said, "You know, maybe we can help you answer some of those questions. Jill has a way of writing and finding helpful answers for people in need and willing to be helped."

"I'm willing to be helped. But if you can find any answers to my mess it'll be a first. What's it like?"

"This is new to us," I explained. "We'll check it out pretty soon and see what comes up. I never know what it will be. I hear, in my ear, the answer to questions and then write it down. I get one word at a time and if I don't write it, no more come. This way I can tell it's not from *me*. I don't know what's coming next. Anyway, it's all I have to offer, so we'll do it."

Table cleared of supper and a pen and paper in my hand we three sat and I wrote.

Thus started the experience of having someone write a few lines and then, as I wrote down the words I heard in my ear, answers were revealed to the seeker.

Jo Long

Home Again

Pearl was driving. We had grown quiet with our own thoughts after saying our farewells to the family we had spent three weeks with. Those people had become precious to us. So much had happened while we were with them. Our knowledge had grown as we shared with everyone we came into contact with. Now we were on our way home.

I broke the silence with, "This has been a trip to remember. We have written for at least forty different people, and they made the opening for us."

"It seemed they made the opening but your writings told you the door would be opened, so that says to me, someone upstairs made the opening. Someone tapped them on the shoulder and they didn't even know it. In fact, must have put words into their minds before they spoke. It was perfect every time.

She smiled. "I think it's one of the greatest miracles of all time. Everyone we touched has had a change of some sort. They know there's more than just the daily ways of living and there's something greater than people. They're wondering how it could be and why they didn't know about it.

"Funny how we all live such different ways. Most of us don't even know ourselves well enough to know why we do certain things. By the way, I'm not criticizing the way my niece Nellie and her family live, but it seems to me they need to be together as a family, in the evenings, during meal time. They never sit at the table as a family. See what the writings have to say about that."

I wrote: "Why doesn't Nellie's family sit at the table to eat their evening meal as a family?"

Due to the many directions and varied hourly chores.

"We feel this togetherness is very important. Is this just an old-fashioned idea?"

For each family a grouping of togetherness is of great importance for deeper understanding. Nellie's time is early morning. Your time is after the evening meal. Nourishment these days can be found in various ways and various places.

"Well! How about that?" I said. "I always feel if I don't get to visit with my family after supper I'm cheated. Art wants the dishes done immediately, but not me. I want to enjoy my family and hear about their day and what they need to do or want to do. I don't care if the dishes are done. Aunt Avis always stacked them and did them when she got breakfast and that's the way I like to do. How 'bout you?"

"I haven't thought about it before, but if my boys weren't home for the supper meal I was upset and they knew they had better be there. No buts. Guess this is learning to know yourself, huh?"

"Well, then, does everyone have a certain time?"

"Ask."

Each has a particular timing of their own. Some are for family. Some are for sleep and others are for necessities of life. Now, you will be aware of the timing for various peoples whom, before, you considered frivolous, because their ways were not your own.

"Now, that's pretty neat. You know, we've learned a lot on this trip. Some of the things asked have been just as helpful to us. How about that bit about Gray's friend being a parasite? Do you think you could find that and just review it?

She had stayed home from school and in her room instead of eating breakfast with the rest of the family. Pearl and I took her a roll and a cup of coffee. Soon she said, "I'm not sick so much as sick at heart. I just don't know what to do and how to handle my life at school. And Mom, well, she doesn't know about the things at school and is too busy to get involved. Do you think I can ask you some questions like the others have been doing? Do you think I could get some answers?"

"Hey!. There's no harm in trying, and the cost is a hug. I'll be back with my pen and paper.

Her first question was, "Why do I dislike Karla so?"

Simple! She is a parasite. Many are of this world. Ones are at guilt to allow this kindness of self to be used. They do the other no favor but dedicate to their shortcomings.

"What does the word 'dedicate' mean as it's used?"
To be dedicated to or let self be used for others convenience and self-avoidance of ill feelings and as you say 'big scene.'
"How can the 'big scene' be avoided?"
By being of charming personality and smiling face, but yet to stand firm in your place.
"My boyfriend. How does he feel about me?"
As a beautiful maiden. He seeks a jolly companion to fill his days of youth. His years indicate a way of freedom but it is a way full of love of life. His days of finding a wife are not yet. Your course is one of same. Enjoy the life of day to day and do not be impatient. Be not his pack donkey of heavy duty and no questions. Step lightly for fear of going over the cliff.

When I re-read these words, I asked her, "Does this have a meaning to you? Is this boy in some sort of trouble with dope? What is he trying to get you to do in the name of love?"

Where in the world did I get such ideas? But her reactions—she covered her face with her hands and said, "Oh my god! Don't tell Mom! She will skin me alive! How did you know he's a part of a group of kids that are selling? They keep wanting me to carry the stuff from the car to the gym. I did it only one time and today they had some more. I want to be with the cool kids, but I was not going to do it. They are not going to get me in their mess of filth. I'm afraid to go against them. What will I do?"

Praise the Lord and ask His deliverance of boyfriend

Marsh. He needs his path directed away from evil and entwined into goodness.

"Can you help word it? I don't know how to do that."

Dear Jesus, spread your light of love to Marsh and shelter him from shame. Pour on me your gracious love and lead us to our home above.

"Oh, thank you. Now I can sleep. I've been crying all night. I didn't know what to do."

While Pearl and I were in her bedroom and she was so needful of our confidence, we did well. But, here in the kitchen we looked at each other in awe. Yes, we wanted to be of help, but to write as she had, that was something! No doubt she needed help. The poor kid. But what would happen when she went to school tomorrow and had to face those people?

Pearl and I were thinking of Grey all the following day. When she came home from school, she motioned us to come upstairs. Her greeting was: "Guess what? Karla and her dopers were picked up by the cops yesterday while I was home in bed! Mash had to spend the night in jail and is out on bond and says he'll never get mixed up in anything like that again. Karla has been shipped off to her dad in Tulsa. I will never have to see her again as long as I live! Isn't that something? And I have you two to thank for it. Oh, how will I ever repay you?"

"No, no, no—not us. God. Say 'Praise the Lord' and give Him the glory. He did these things. We just wrote what I heard and showed you there was more in this world available than what you can see. And we're sure glad to be

Council of Angels

used in such a wonderful way."

"I can't believe it!" she continued. "All the kids were talking about it. Cops were all over the place, going through the lockers and desks. They had the dogs and everything. I wanted to come home at noon and tell you, but I was afraid you would be gone. Isn't it something? I can live my life again and, believe me, no parasite will take advantage of me no matter how popular or how good looking." She laid her head down on her crossed arms and muttered to herself, "God, how good it is to be free of them!"

Reviewing this event left us in ten minutes of silence as we drove down the road. "Well," said Pearl, "several got a message in that one."

"Yeah. Lives were changed with that miracle." I flipped through the stack of papers. "How about this one? Nellie said this woman's husband is a mule, but she called him a little something more appropriate."

Pearl laughed. "Ask."

To have a team move a load up a tall hill is to pull as lead mule indicates.

"When I wrote those words, I actually visualized two mules pulling a heavy wagon. One mule was pulling to the right and the other to the left—pulling the single tree, the piece of harness, apart—and not getting up the hill. This visualization was new for me, but it certainly made a clear picture as to the impossibility of a team pulling a load when not pulling together toward a mutual goal."

"How about trust? I loved that one. It actually made me

feel rich. Read it."

I shuffled through the papers until I found the answer.

Pray as directed. Trust us to be doing our works you set in motion. That is to say, Jesus I've spent my energy and leave this in your keeping. Then think of it no more for if you put your diamonds in the giant vault, do you not know of their safe keeping? Then trust no less your treasures in God's keeping and sing him praises for he smiles upon your joyful countenance. His vault is the largest of all.

Pearl nodded. "Once we put our prayer in God's keeping we are to leave it there. Not take it back and keep worrying with it as people usually do."

"Yeah, and make our prayer specific and detailed and we had best be careful what we pray for—we might get it. Then, too, there is that waiting period of three days after one makes their commitment to have God in their life. Like when I prayed for Chigger and the next three days he was a little devil on wheels. That can be a time of giving up on believing there's a God.

"Here's one I like: '. . .*We are your Guardian Angels of protection; your scouts and your answers to doubt, your personnel advisors, your ramrods and directors. . . .There are many angels on various missions. . . .Many [of us] are unassigned and are in state of waiting. As said before, your actions put us to action. Until we are put to action we. . . wait. . . .Long have I been with you and happy to be of added service. Now we complete our cycle of involvement and thus grow as you grow. Your comforter is as a*

Council of Angels

guardian angel to a small child, but at time of adulthood our hands are tied. Since a time of development has been reached, you aware of me. As one is aware of their guardian angel in youth, it is for them to be aware of the same in adulthood, but to become aware of the source available is the key.

"Can you help us to understand the duties of God, Jesus and the Holy Spirit? Some say they are the same. Yet all through the Bible it talks as if they are three different beings. I have had ministers explain them as compared to an egg. The shell, the white and the yoke. Each of these have a different function and value and I can see how none can work with out the other but I have never been able to understand The Three."

God is all. All knowledge, all love and all beauty. All mans' fulfillment and contentedness.

Jesus, son of God, inheritor of all and perfected in bodily form of man to show man free obedience to God and the Bible.

Holy Spirit is power of the universe used for betterment of mankind.

Comforter is the spirit of Christ, implanted in each, awaiting acceptance and thus releasing the powers of the Holy Spirit to do the works of Jesus for mans' salvation and acceptance of God's pleasures through. . .a road to goodness through immovable odds. To have the comforter active is also full acceptance and use of all things through Jesus from God.

"When I have prayed for other's health I have only said

the prayer I hear in my ear."

This is how you pray through the Holy Spirit to reach the realm of God. Those who pray to Jesus are themselves going to the realm of God. . . .You call upon Jesus to descend upon you the active Holy Spirit and send the knowledge of the comforter to divulge the words to God who hears and answers. . . these actions are as sure as the rising of the sun and the turning of the earth. . . .To have access to the knowledge of the universe is to have found the correct ways of God.

"It seems to me this is a difficult way of finding out how to pray. Why make it so hidden."

Due to mans' lack of desire for perfection, he must seek to locate the treasures laid aside for his use. To come easy has small meaning.

I looked at Pearl. "We're learning, and we can use this in our own lives, but we'll have to remember to remember." I closed the notebook. "It will be good to get home from this wonderful trip. We should be there in about three more hours.

Council of Angels

Ramona's Story

It was great to be home. It seemed as if I had been gone three months instead of three weeks. There were many things to get caught up on. But to my surprise, there were friends here who wanted answers, too. The grapevine line had been busy. The very first week home, a friend brought Ramona to me asking asking if I could be of help to her. I wrote: "Ramona is here asking for guidance in her life. We are ready for your suggestions."

Clearly, came these words: *Now has come time for decisions. To know what she is searching for is our first step. Her salvation is the ultimate, but what is salvation? It is a way of knowing her God. For it is through Him she finds reason for life, contentment and confidence in self as it is meant to be. Her life has been one of upheaval and emptiness. Now we come to this phase of living—to set courses in mid-stream. . .for the light has shown souls care who share a mutual love.*

Ramona asked: "What are the souls who share a mutual love?"

Son and husband. She is their mutual love.

"Should I change my way of living?"

Ramona knows she is not living as God nor society means man and woman should live. Mort is not blind either. Why then do they find a bondage to one another, for he is not she, nor she he, yet as we share the nights lodging do we become only a part of the other.

"How can I change this? Do I really love him?"

Can a mother truly love any being who is not gentle, kind and considerate to her child? For naught will come of such an acquaintance.—Waste no more puny hours on a puff of air for where he is going he does not care. He can not get to heaven if he asks not. . . .All the gifts await those who believe and ask to be received, but if they care not how can He care more? He is a wanderer—has no sail nor his own ship. She has her ship in her children and a sail she is to get.

"Should I give him up?"

We are very slow to give up on a soul, but no slower than she. Here are two roads of travel for their's is not a love but a tryst and a need. It has become an empty burden on each of them.

"How is it a burden on Mort?"

In his inadequacy of providing the worldly needs for self and blossom. For he is not help in any way and he can see this. He can only wallow in the mire.

As I read what I had written I asked Ramona: "What

does this mean to you? It makes no sense to me."

She looked a little embarrassed. "Well, yes, it makes sense to me. 'Blossom' is what he calls me. It's his pet name for me. He says he can call me Blossom, because I'm his blooming idiot. She looked away, her face tense. "He doesn't provide for me. We live in my trailer. I buy the groceries from my money and I even buy his beer and cigarettes. He really doesn't provide for me at all. The car is mine, too, and because it's mine, he says I should buy the gasoline and pay for the insurance and upkeep of it. He has a good job and a big pay check, but deposits it in the bank in his savings account—in his name only." She paused. "And he doesn't want my children around."

"Hmmmmm," was my only comment.

"Ask what would be the easiest way to get rid of him," she urged.

What is easy? But is is not easy in this manner either. In standing alone a light has shown—Peace of mind will flow in actions of right—do not despair for I'll be there and guide you in the night. It is not a matter of time, but of learning. Her desire to improve is a shock he needs.

Ramona asked: "Should I rededicate my life to the church?"

Not necessarily, but to be present in the house of the Lord is important. To find your church house in my name be very careful, for you are over supplied with many false prophets and misconceptions. So be particular of the church for my sake. Man is not made to want others to know the things they show is not so. What you write is for the individual alone for doubts and fears one has if they do not know to reach out and rid those for, again I tell you we can only sit on a rock and wait our presence to partake. For you to accept the full impact of your prayers from God through Jesus can be equated to a horse's kick. Again I tell you, for us to interfere in one's life is not of our choice, but the choice of the individual or through the loving gift from another. We are ever present, like the moon and stars—by light of day are of out of sight to man.

Ramona asked: "And what do you mean 'the living gift from another'?"

There can be no greater gift than the prayer offered secretly by a caring person. This is a loving gift from another.

Another friend brought someone wanting help.

She did not know how far they should go in helping their son. She asked if they could help him further.

Not if they are not ready to help themselves.

Judge not least ye be judged does not mean you have no control nor knowledge of right or wrong. For if you see a man do wrong, shout the knowledge and feeling of wrong doing. Judge not his soul but his actions and hold him not in contempt. God is to condemn or redeem. . . .

Now, can you force the wind
to blow the leaves
to a cooling breeze?
Can you raise the sun
and cause water not to run

Council of Angels

Can you feel the heat
and say be cool
Nor can you change
a loved one from a fool

Attuned to the powers is a way to radiance. Attuned to God is to be attuned to the powers. Attuned to the life's cycles of evolution is attuned to the cosmic powers. Knowledge is a growth. Knowledge is using intelligently the laws of the universe for betterment. Knowledge is broadening one's outlook and developing oneself in. . . understanding existing powers. Knowledge, if stored in a stone jar closed from light only lies in wait 'till someone opens the jar or breaks it, causing the knowledge to. . .grow to a tremendous tree of ever-lasting bloom to share— all the radiance of bloom and smell of sweetness. Knowledge to share outgrows the original jar and demands a larger, more appropriate one, soon again to grow beyond all containers and be free in the world.

"How do I achieve higher goals for myself and family?"

Yourself. Not family.

In attaining higher. . .goals, the family finds enrichments and prestige. Goals and improvements are a personal thing.

"O.K. But how?"

First: Accomplishment of. . .tasks.
Second: Answering 'Call to arms' in faith
Third: Cast off chains of limitations that bind you. Let

powers become the lights of the universe and apply them to heal the bodily functions. . .excess energy will soon be the reward.

"I know my daily tasks. . . .Am I to decide what I want to be?"

Have your footsteps led you to your destination? No. As for wife, mother and grandmother, yes. But to soar to heights unknown. . .is a progress anew. Now, unfurl your wings and let nothing impede your way. . . .

"Is feeling cosmic power like feeling the power of the Holy Spirit?"

No—The birth of a baby, the sting of a bee.
The fear of a hurricane, and the feel of spring rain,
The source of life's powers, the twist of fate
The cause of pain is always great

To be in charge of your life's stream
Is all of goodness, like a sweet dream
To filtrate slowly, life's knowledgeable ways
Takes painful learning of many days
To become aware is a learning process
Herein keeping your life from a mess
The Holy Spirit is of Divine Guidance
And never a stress

"Then the feeling of cosmic powers are not always good?"

They are the laws of force to the entire. . .universe. This is too great for measured comprehension. Painful, beautiful and never ceasing to be, as days on days and assurance of night fall. Here there is no pain at all. . .does love have no pain—is it all the same? Do the fields of beauty produce grain? Let all tests be likened to a board.

"You mean the laws never bend?"

Again—it is the way, night or day.

"The book I bought yesterday, *Cosmic Magnetism*. . . ."

All in the universe is from or of God. There are laws of effort and effect. If you school yourself in the best knowledge and use no other ways, the effects of your actions will be good and good heaped on good reaps good thus acquiring an abundance of good in possessions and in love to and from others.

To learn application of the laws is to improve.

"I believe I understand. It's the good feeling of self achievement."

February '75.

"Who is 'The Father?'"

The Father. . .as you refer is God in spirit and is the creator of mankind. In Jesus, son of God, do we discover the actual teacher of man and thus inheritor also of title 'Father.' All things are from God, through the Son, The Father and The Holy Spirit. Here, as in 'The Lord's Prayer' they are the one and only to which prayer is directed.

"I must turn on music and do my housework. Don't

know why I feel low—am I causing this myself? So much to do."

By being in doubt of which way to turn you lose the peace for which you yearn. Doubt not and never—we are beside you ever to guide, confide. . . .go forward into the new ways and eagerly. Let past ways remain in the past. Joy and action puts all in proper stance and soon. . .in the mind, only achievements. Endure.

Accomplishment is a spiritual and visual thing. Together are the paths of progress doubled. . . .to do a thing is to start wheels—many—to turn. Let not hours be wasted in darkness of doubt and fear of gloom but in smiles and thankfulness enjoy each minute, at that minute, and let worries become hazards of past pathways. Grasp this. . . . Let it become a part of you for herein lies energy, strength, knowledge in all solutions and tranquillity among all you touch. Vouchsafe. The day awaits.

Council of Angels

A Leap Forward

Monday, 8:20 a.m. "Slowly getting some small things done. Any words?"

Delaying and working at a slow pace are not the same. Accomplishments can be met at slow pace. . . .you did not get the meaning of Saul and Samuel? How about this? Those selected for kingship were expected to be among the prominent. But—not as 'they' expected—but in humbleness and knowledgeable ways of labor. . . .So it is yet. Saul lived many lives and saved many lives. He led where the Lord said. Saul was a giant among his people, but a servant of God. He led many in the Lord's footsteps and left the world a better place. . . .The Lord had use of him for many years and filled his lands with honey and lotus. . . .in abundance. Many were the children of Israel who rebuked him in his position and action, yet he knew not all were searchers or followers of God, but condemned them not. . . .

"This is way out of my category. I know little about Bible stories. I'm willing to learn, though. Thank you."

Tuesday, 8:10 a.m. "Today is cooler and cloudy. I've

no special plans."

Much can be your's this day. Surrender personal desires and stress helpfulness to those who present themselves. Waiting is nearly over and harvesting nearly begun. Sing the songs of gladness and tarry no more in ways of rejoicing, for near at hand is the higher ground on which to stand.

"I want to go back to bed, but guess I'd better dress for company. Is my fatigue today my imagination?"

Put on music. No fatigue is due to starving tissue. . . . Use juice of meats, capsules of E and complex of B. Cranapple juice aides the toxic condition. Rest. Respond at time of demand.

But I gave in to my feelings. I put my nightgown on and went to bed. If someone wanted me, they would have to let me know.

My friend down the block rang the door bell at ten. We had coffee and toast.

Our oldest daughter telephoned to tell me they were doing fine financially, and in school and health wise. All was fine! Good news. I'm so grateful.

Wed. 8:30 a.m. . . .meditation is fine—but prayer is what you do. . . .you feel as past days were wasted, yet the message from your daughter was one of complete happiness. . . .Your friend's was one of true companionship. Where then is the emptiness? All of this while you mend. Also joyful fulfillment of another goal set and met with no apparent stress. . .$80.00 for bills. Also joyous news of son, and wife and boys. All happy reports and thoughtful *gestures...today will you receive strength to accomplish all you set out to do and joyful will be your day.*

"Dear Father, so blind are we to our blessings. I could not sum my day up so beautifully. I am grateful for your presence in our lives and the peace, faith and contentment we have now. How great to know you. Still so much to do!"

All is of a secured nature. Only your desires of enjoyment yet remain....

Sometimes, when all is secure, is a span of readjusting to secure feeling. Be at ease.

Retreat to cozy comforts to repair. At times of need there must be time for repair first. Each person has freedom of choice. One choice leads to unhappiness and confusion. Another to peace of mind and satisfaction. Evaluate situation.

Heed my warnings and adjust lifestyle to rotate around my realm of learning. To justify is to excuse and to comply is to harvest a greatness and endurance.

"Where do I start?"

By first saying 'yes' then putting actions into being.
Up at 6:00 a.m.

"Am I to get up a 6:00 a.m. to write every morning?"

And stay up 'til fatigue compels you to rest—then again and again. Soon rest will become less and less, then little, for much time will be in enjoyable actions in my name, putting proper undertakings into being.

Fantasy is great but seldom advantageous. To assemble a gathering of interested people is first to find such people. To find people of interest is our task. To be prepared to teach these people is your's and to be ever diligent in searching answers is your's. Do not hesitate to complete small tasks set and do compel onward to the next task that seems to make itself apparent. Let these manifest themselves and thus approaching their solving will eliminate any indecision on your part.

"How do I teach others when I need so many answers?"

By listening. Also from past and present experiences. Just lean on faith and encourage actions.

"You will have to speak loud and clear!"

You have always heard before. Go in tranquillity. I am with you always. Go where you feel is right and there will I be also.

"After talking to one of my friends and hearing her tell about their Bible-study class I realized how little I knew of the Bible. I need the words and locations of so many things in the Bible. Yet, in another way, I have them through you. This is my first day to be here at 6:00 a.m."

Locate in 1 Samuel, Chapters 12 and 15. read it.

"What is this about?"

Battles. First was great confusion and God's people won over many odds. Next Matthew 16.

"I'm not retaining this. Hard to understand it."

All will fill proper segments soon. Now turn to I Samuel again.

"Chapter 16: Samuel pleads for forgiveness. God chooses David to be Samuel's body guard."

Let not your heart be troubled—so many things of

learning to come. But slowly it shell be done.

Putting people equal to animals is, in a way, an injustice to the animals. Yet, to lower man to the secondary stage is to not let God's works be justified. Each has their place in the realm of God's creation and each is a perfection in itself. So let us then assume God's plan is perfect and mans' laws a necessity. . . .More need to show love now and be made aware of it than ever before.

"Why?"

. . . .Necessities have caused man to become unfeeling to another's needs and thus even to his own needs. To feel again is our desire. For feelings cannot be captured in an iron box nor a test tube, but it is an unseeing and unformed thing of great, great importance. To feel is to be. To be is to be felt and to be felt is to know the care of God.

Forming judgments are not in good standing. Undesirables are in judgments of man, based on mans' code or law. God's eyes find different windows. They are windows to the soul. Mans' eyes only seek windows of reflections and always these are an elusive thing—as shadows—they cannot withstand strong light. Train your eyes to cast off the show and see, instead, the more lasting image. Put away all secondary light and travel only with the bright light of mid-day. Then all shadow will be cast away and only true images remain for you. Intent is rampant. Done and doing are more easily recognized and are true actions.

"You have said 'intent' is rampant?"

. . .actions with ill intent. . .cannot be called 'impulsive'.

...Intent put to...action causes deliberate ill gains. . . . to let this go undetained is...to condone these actions and spur the doer onward undetained. Stop these doers when they cross your path and rebuke them in their actions, then hold them accountable no more. God condemns and redeems.

The following week. "This is my 4th day in a row of feeling good. It's great! Wonderful! Last evening I got home from a full day of sales and got supper immediately.

Later the same day. "My house chores are nearly done and I still feel great! Can I hear from you or am I being a bother?"

Is a soft spring breeze a bother
Are early blossoms on the trees a bother
Are sparkling melodies of a brook a bother
Nor is loves faith and trust a bother

"I love these verses!"

Some days we slave and never care
Some days it seems we get no where
Some days we thrill to achievements met
Some days we only come home spent

Here is a gift from me to you
Here is a way to see you through
Here is a small token of renown
To let you know you own a crown

"I love it! Any more?"

A rose can only bloom once
The petals fade and fall
By giving of ourselves
Kindness, care and thoughtfulness
A garden grows forever
Its beauty never rests

"Now I'm ready to get back to my chores."
Ready yourself for the next step of achievement.
"What will that be?"
You will see. The time is not yet. Rest.

Council of Angels

The Council

March 11, 1976:

8:00 a.m. My family were still gathering their things as they left for school. I went to my customary chair on the east side of the living room and took my book and pen in hand. I started my day by saying "The Lord's Prayer" after printing the "P."

Immediately I became aware of others in the room with me. Looking around, I could see no one. Thinking it must be the presence of my family still in the house I ignored the feeling. But vaguely, I was aware of the door slamming and knew my family was gone.

No longer could this feeling of others in the room be ignored. In fact, the room was *full*. I froze. I was stunned. Oh-oh! Here I go again! Now what's happening?

Slowly, I shifted my eyes to the left. There, on the arm of the couch, sat a figure I had never seen before. I couldn't move. I could hardly breath. I could see him, yet I could see *through* him. He wore a navy-blue, pin-strip suit, a bowler hat and a cane was jauntily swinging from his arm. He was extremely personal. About six foot in height, with a lean, oval face around clear, blue eyes. He was smiling in a gentle, patient and understanding way. His hands were beautifully manicured and his shoes were well polished beneath gray spats. (I recalled my father wearing spats many years ago, but these days no one wore spats!) This "person" was dressed impeccably. He was perfectly at ease. He was in no hurry and was obviously waiting to be recognized.

I never felt so naked in my life, although I was fully dressed. This person *knew* every thing about me. Every secret I *thought* I ever had.

Slowly, as if watching a Polaroid film develop, I saw another figure in the middle of the couch, on the center cushion. A man with white hair. His face was smooth, and cherubic, with radiant features—full of energy. He wore a plain gray suit and no hat but a cane was casually resting beside him.

The thin man sitting next to him, was an altogether different type. His dark hair was combed smooth to his scalp and he wore a black, turtle-neck sweater. His trousers were of a black, shiny material and he had comfortable slippers on his feet. He seemed to be carrying a short cane. On closer look, it was not a cane, but a baton.

Sitting on the west side of the room directly facing me was my piano and in front of it was the piano stool. On it I could see only parts of a man. He had his arms crossed on his crossed knee. I could see his wrists and fingers—from the knees down to and including the feet and well polished

Council of Angels

shoes of black leather.

I realized I was breathing through my gaping mouth, but I was too amazed to move. Each of these had very slowly developed one after the other. I decided I was really balmy now! My mind was doin' over time. I, somehow, had conjured these things up from my wild, bizarre, active imagination. But why did I only see the bottom half of the man on the piano stool? If I tried really hard I could dream up the rest of him, couldn't I? I would like to see all of him. Try as I might, I could not develop any more of that body. What the heck! What's goin' on?, I wondered.

With that last thought, came an answer. The figure, that's all I can call him, spoke, except there was *no sound*. The figures were quiet, like fog. Never before had I realized there was actually *sound* accompanying a human body. The figure on my left communicated to me, not verbally, but as in my writing, I heard his voice only in my inner ear.

I am your constant companion. Some would refer to me as your guardian angel. I have been with you since time began. I am with you day and night to guide you in all ways and to assist in any endeavor. I can be refereed to as Flynn.

He was debonair. I was embarrassed in his presence. He knew me. Even more than I knew myself. Nooo, no no no. Not like an acquaintance, I mean he *knew* me. Every little detail. *And* thought. *And* desire. *And* dream. This guy had my number!

The next man, in a gray suit and with white hair, was

divulging, *I am your comforter, your doctor, your psychiatrist, your special aid in times of all needs in the physical respect. I am Mason.*

He was soft spoken, confident and reassuring. I could believe he was capable of correcting any emergency.

Then, the third man spoke. Like the others, he didn't exactly speak, but I got the message anyway.

He was about six foot one or two, very thin and more business like.

You may know me as Rene, poet, composer, artist and stenographer.

"Are you for me personally? I mean only for me?"

Why not? Development is great and those in other areas are not aware of the availability.

"Why are you all men?"

We are not men. We are entities. . .we have volunteered . . . .Here, time is no problem and rush-rush is never. We propel at a comfortable rate and do indulge ourselves with pleasantness of comfort and convenience. . . .But our terrestrial bodies are made to be revealed at opportunities.

From number four, which was only seen as the hands resting crossed at the wrists on the knee of the crossed legs, *I am here to overcome physical discords and to rejuvenate and recycle—to utilize to fulfillment.*

Number one spoke again. I am your constant companion, guide, personnel relations, repair man and tailor; repairer of appliances, cars, calculators, blenders and household arrangements.

I shook my head. This was too much.

Council of Angels

Number 3 chimed in. *And am I the author, poet, artist, composer and literary guide. . .your development on this one sphere is nearly complete. These others are perhaps more discreet and just as available. . . .Be content in knowledge spent as in $ and cents. Soon will be need of further developments on your part and then these others will be at your disposal.*

I was interrupted by my telephone ringing. After answering it, I started doing my day's work. I steered clear of the living room. I had had all of the shock I could take for one day. No, I didn't forget the experience, but was too leery to give anymore time to the examination of the happening. I loaded my sales merchandise into the car and was off to appointments one hundred and twenty miles away.

Jo Long

Holding Fast

My sales business took me to many places. I gave home parties, met customers in beauty shops or any place which offered private and one-on-one contact.

For this appointment, by the time I closed with my hostess, it was 1:00 a.m. I was accustomed to these late-night treks home and my car was pretty reliable. The gasoline tank was full. My heater and defroster worked. As I put my merchandise in the car, the moon peeked between the black swiftly-moving clouds. It was beautiful. The wind was about twenty miles per hour with an icy chill.

I had the road to myself. At this time of night, in the country, that was to be expected. With nearly half the miles toward home covered, sprinkles of rain blurred my windshield. I turned on the wipers. No response. It was as if they were disconnected.

Oh oh! I thought. This is no time to have my wipers go out. If it doesn't rain any harder than this I can see well enough. But this condition lasted only a short time. Soon the drops were huge and blinded my way to the extent that

Council of Angels

I was crawling along at a dangerously low speed. I did not dare pull off the highway onto the shoulder. It would be muddy and I could get stuck. What to do? I thought. "Well, this is where I could use some of that unseen help I've been writing about." I said outloud. "How bout it? Are you guys out there? If you are, get this windshield wiper goin'. I need to get home safely."

I reached for my wipers again and pulled them on. No go. I pushed them off. I drove a few miles further and again in desperation I pulled the wiper button. They worked! Oh my gosh! I thought. I'm not going to touch them again. Must be a loose connection. But if it was a loose connection, why did thy come on at all? Or if there is not a loose connection, why didn't they work in the first place? Oh well, I thought, if they just keep working I'll make it home.

I got home with my wipers going strong, went inside my house and crawled in bed for a few hours sleep before getting up to see my family off.

I forgot to tell Art about my windshield wipers in the bustle of the morning. I didn't tell him about the spirits, either.

After finishing my dishes and a couple cups of coffee in the quiet of the house I thought about my trip home. Then about the visions of the spirits in my living room. I decided I had to take time to write. "The visions revealed to me—are they from my own mind?"

Ah-haa! So—first, let us see the mind.
Mind: Source of all form of knowledge, reason, fear,

doubt, love. Now, thru the mind is access to all. We on this level of being appear in bodily form except we do not have any of the bodily handicaps—need of food, rest, heat, nor transport. We can become 'apparent' in times of necessity and to transport our bodies is not a problem. We go by thought waves and time is no handicap for we are timeless. . . . .You realize now the importance in dress, being ready. Always you've judged 'time enough to get ready'. . . .Here there is none. . . .removing the idea of 'maybe' or 'when'.

"Oh! So, O.K. now what?"

Number 5 has not been revealed to you. Here is a reason for slowly developing the inner sight. To be aware of other entities on the outer premises is—for they are ever present—to know to reject them as unacceptable for you—reason enough for slower training in ways of goodness.

"Are these parts of *my* personality conjured up into forms by me?"

Never. Here could have been 'personalities you wished to become' or even 'personalities you have known in this life and admired' or 'people you've known in this life or your other lives.

All are no. We have, each of us at one time or another, lived our lives on earth. That's why we can understand all your feelings. No—we never lived at your time of living. We were before. No, none of us are a part of you—your 'personality' will be none of us. Knowledge is what we impart and understanding comes thru knowledge.

"Well, it seems to me I am very slow in adjusting my life to improvement. And in accepting. You know this is pretty much. Anyone else will think I'm balmy. So do I, at times."

You have so many areas going at once. We've kept you on schedule and you have complied well. You expect decades to unfold before your very eyes and we must gear you to your physical capacity.

"I feel you can cure me of every ill and physical malfunction if you want to. Comment?"

I ate, instead of waiting for an answer. I was not ready to take on any more of this quick knowledge. I started my dishes and put my first load in the washer; picked up the odds and ends strewn around and became exhausted thinking about the many other little things of wifely chores. Fold the clothes. Start supper. Finally I returned to the chair and again picked up my pen. It was as if I had never left the room. The message continued where I had left off.

Well, not in your ideas. Miracles are happening all the time. For instance. The season's change will be soon. Man will not call it so but God will. Man will call it most unusual, what it has never been before. To heal is as always. The threads of repair are great. Yes, in time your bodily repairs will be noticed. A lot of man's works are of physical nature and in physical actions does his bodily repair come about.

"Is this the way I will repair?"

For now.

"Who helps me with these endless chores of household and clothing?"

It is #1 and #2.

"Well, I must not be listening well enough for I'm not responding. How can I do better?"

By relying on #1.

"I cannot feature #1 cleaning house and planning meals."

His capabilities are and his enjoyment in so doing. #2 is steadfast reliable and confident. #3 is also of a needed nature. As each area develops to a competent stage and necessity arises, will they each then be revealed.

Metering out movements may seem not-educating to some but first tasks to master are the menial ones of everyday living of bodily care and functions. Unless these are out of the way the environment is cluttering the mind and hinders any directional reception. As tasks fly by is time also to think, plan and praise the Lord for here is a way to 'kill 2 birds with one stone'. Soon depression will be as was fear—a past way of life. . .and then open highways of spaciousness.

"Well, I submitted to fear this morning at the post office when I got the bankruptcy letter from our company's lawyer. But it was only information as to the way the procedures were going. I was shown how awful was the way of fear as it used to be. I'm grateful for such a tremendous improvement in all our lives. For some of it has reached even the most distant of our family."

Yes, and yearning also has diminished—not true desire, but yearning comes from discontent. Do continue your wee chores. Put on music to glide you through.

Council of Angels

A Richer Life

The end of the week I met Pearl at the Half-way Cafe to pick up product and to enjoy a visit. We were busy in our own ways but always interested in each other's lives. Our friendship was a thing we could mutually rely on. After the two-hour lunch and exchange of life's events we separated for our homes. I had only gone a few miles when I felt the urge to write. I pulled into a parking lot.

"Have some time and I just want to hear from you?"

Be it said of your many achievements: There is one well done. Far more nearly perfect than all the rest—that of the act of 'friendship' for here is giving, caring, feeling needs of and understanding. Here is trust, faith, fellowship, content and enjoyment. Here is appreciation for endeavors, appreciation of sharing and interest in mutual acquisition. Herein lies a jewel selection for your crown of gold. Rubys, diamonds, amethyst and jades. All amply placed amidst pearls and sapphires to shine from your brow—for all to be aware of. Sincerity is among the greatest of these and sprinkled with small diamonds in the midst of a background of pure gold holds all who are aware in greatest awe.

I was overcome! What a treasure. How did I arrive at this stage—to hear and actually see entities of help?

By your desire for knowledge and your continual quest.

The rest of my trip home I sang at the top of my lungs. Ha! I was so happy.

The very next morning I got bills in the mail. In near panic I wrote.

"We don't have enough money to pay our bills. I took one hundred dollars and ordered merchandise with it. It was not enough to pay the bills anyway. Now I need money to pay the telephone bill: $70.34, CIPS: $41.00, and taxes: $83.00, so I really need help here. Is there a way?"

At last are the bonds of independence cast aside and supervision requested. Continue in the paths of content but intent to accomplish—set goals, resist confusion and continue upswing process of actions. Apply self to actions. Final.

The following morning when I got up I felt so wonderful! At 8:00 a.m. I wrote:

Praise the Lord. What a beautiful day. "Any message?"

Many are the messages and much is the need. Only desire needs to be stronger.

#1 is: Blessed are they who seek for they shall find.

#2: Blessed are they who desire truth and righteousness for they shall be leaders of men.

Council of Angels

#3: Blessed are the meek for they shall inherit the earth. Beatitudes are many. Understanding small and further study seems of a childish nature. Yet to read and re-read is accepted. Let's study them. 'Matthew: 5: 3-12,' 'Luke: 6:20-22.'

"This is really the beatitudes. What a wonderful way to find them to study."

12:30—A letter arrived from my brother who farmed a few acres of land for me. I had a corn check for $660. I subtract the years expenses of $253.47 and $406.53! I can pay our bills! Or put $400 on our loan. "Which?"

You asked for money to pay bills.

"O.K. pay bills it is. What to do with the rest?"

We suggest paying 200.00 on the loan, making a sizable advance. The purchase of added merchandise will be from another source. A noticeable cushion to draw from for needs not yet seen.

What a way of life! How wonderful! Thank you— Praise the Lord! Praise the Lord! Praise the Lord!

Oh! I want to shout our good fortune to the world—for all to hear. "Who can I tell? Anyone?"

Enjoy your fruits and sing praises of glory. Soon now others will see and know your story.

Three days later I woke with the sniffles and a sore throat

"Why did I get this cold? Have I failed tests?"

As failure to regenerate is. . .so follows malfunctions of bodily achievements. To comply to laws of nature in care of the body is to reap readiness and aptness of bodily functions. Rely on us. Each act and re-action is either of us or against us—test. Ask results and obey only the profitable.

"O.K. For a cold it is honey and vinegar. Lemons and bullion instead of coffee, and *rest*. How do I get thru this party tonight?"

Say Praise the Lord and press onward.

"Praise the Lord for my bad health. Praise the Lord for my heavy body. Praise the Lord for my arthritis. Praise the Lord for my aches and stiffness. Praise the Lord for my weaknesses and desire for food. Praise the Lord for this cold. I've a prayer of thanksgiving just for knowing you and for knowing even the small bit I know about you. Now, any messages?"

Always I am near and all powers are mine. Release your ills and rejoice in the Lord.

"I thought I had! Give me the strength to be rid of my doubts."

I just relaxed and went to bed, I was so tired. Then, as if on a huge screen, I saw myself in a beautiful green pasture, the grasses were stirred by a warm gentle breeze. Spring daisies sprinkled their beauty and in the lower part was a stream of perfectly clear water. The sky was a soft baby blue and the feeling was of perfect peace—a quietness beyond any I had ever known. This was Heaven. The perfection could belong to no other. I met Jesus there, although I don't know what he looked like. I handed him a basket of my ills, including my cold. Then I came back down here to my house. It seems I longed for constant lingering in such a meadow but I had tasks to do.

"Is this as it should be?"

A gathering of many is in effect and thru glimpses of Heaven do you receive strength and knowledge to continue on course set, and yet by knowing of such a vastness of meadow beauty can you continue to lead others to such beauty. So continue your daily schedule and commit it's glory to us. Amen.

Two days later made an entry in my journal.

"Had Pat's party last night and took in $180. Night before cleared $70, and booked two more parties. Today, Art took me to the Doctor and I have allergies. Am on medicine. Need to take it easy and skip work for a while. I am so miserable it will not be too hard. Think I'm gonna sleep for a week."

I didn't sleep for a week but it took several days of mostly rest and small amounts of work in the house to get to feeling better. This was nothing unusual for me. I would go to the point of exhaustion, day and night, and then take a few days to recuperate.

However! With all of this new found knowledge—I expected to be zapped well—to not have to go through the same ol' way of recovering from a cold.

Don't work that way. There are still the laws of nature that will never change.

Jo Long

My Time

March 26, 1975.
This was a special day. My birthday. The family remembered and at breakfast had shown their love with various gifts. I was feeling appreciated as I ushered each of them off to school.

Now I could have my quiet time and meditative writing.

Contentedly, I sat in my chair and held my book and pen at ready. Then I realized I was not alone. The room had other occupants. I sat very still. Hardly breathing. I was aware of the three to my left who always sat on the davenport. But the one, I could previously only see part of, and who usually sat on the piano stool, was slowly becoming more visible, like the development of a Polaroid film. Now I could see his upper arms, shoulders and neck. Finally, the outline of the head, the hair. And last, but so detailed, was his face. Square chin, smiling lips, soft round cheeks and bright alert eyes topped with gray, wavy hair. I knew his name was Harper. He was my alchemist. He sat as

Council of Angels

if waiting to see if I would greet him. I felt very comfortable with his presence and was eager to learn what ever he had to teach me. I had no idea what an alchemist was.

Next, to his left, which would be on the north side of my living room and on the arm of a chair was a figure with fire red hair and his face was sprinkled with many freckles. He was aggressive and overbearing. I didn't feel comfortable with him and I thought, "Oh no. This won't do. I could never work with you."

He was disappointed, but I was positive he and I would never make friends. He appeared as if coming into the room again and *again* I thought, "Huh-uh. No way!"

The third time he came in, he also relayed the thought information that he would be my cook. Again, I refused his presence. He drifted away and out of sight.

In his place came another. This one had dark hair, a gentle nature and was of French descent. I could accept him as my cook. His name was Felix.

Sitting next to him was Ben. I knew instantly he and I had already been working together but now was he revealed to me. Of course I didn't recognize his looks, I had never seen him before. It was the feel of his personality that I recognized. I was totally shocked! This person had helped me with my orders in business and in the arrangements of articles in my inventory. He was my financial adviser, business partner, accountant and anything else I needed in the fields of business. Wow!

Ben was a very business-like person of middle age. He did not seem to ridicule my inability in business matters, but was there to help, which I needed. His suit was navy blue and he wore hush-puppy shoes. Very up to date!

Next to him was another man, one with the air of fun. This middle-age man was neatly dressed in a dark blue suit. His hair was dark,too, and so were his eyes. The hands were the focal point. They were soft, tapered and capable. He related to me that he was called "Freed" and said:

I am here to free you from slavery of drudge. To take stress out of chores. You will know of my presence in the flecks in the sunbeams. You call them dust particles. No more. For it will be as a gift of aid in your housekeeping, dishwashing and arrangements of home. In the uncluttering of the accumulations and in the goals set before you. This is as great a gift as one can receive—you think. Ha! All the small tasks will fly and the achievements will be many.

The next person was sitting in the chair beside me. He was of extremely thin stature and wore a dark suit, with a clerical collar. Obviously, church type. He was my Doctor of Theology—a theologian. He *knew* what was in the Bible, and the differences in the many religions of the world. They were *many*. He was a complete encyclopedia set. Now, I had eight helpers.

#1 was Flynn; Constant companion, Guardian, Guide.

#2 was Mason; Comforter, Doctor,

#3 was Rene; Poet, artist, designer, composer and painter

#4 was Harper; Alchemist

Council of Angels

#5 was Felix; Cook
#6 was Ben; Business consultant
#7 was Freed; Freedom of drudge in all things.
#8 was Gallenkemp; Theologian, Scholar, Teacher.
As I wrote their names they faded into nothingness

In a stunned silence, I sat perfectly still. I wasn't frightened. Awed, astounded, dumfounded and wondering about my sanity could more describe my feeling. It did run through my mind that I should be scared out of my wits. But I was not. Naked! Yeah, naked to the marrow of my bones; the deeper most parts of my brain, but fully clothed. This was a different kind of naked. This was an *inside* kind of nakedness. An inside of me I never knew existed. My mind was alert. I even felt more naked than the first time I saw these people.

No one will ever believe this. They will say: What have you been drinking? Or What are you high on? I have never used drugs in my life and I don't drink anything stronger than *Pepsi*. No explanation here. Nor, do I have insanity in my family history. Well, how did it happen?

I sat still trying to figure it out. As I looked—and I do mean looked—at each of the now unoccupied seats, I could see absolutely nothing except the furniture. As had become my action when lacking understanding, I wrote: What is this?

Committee of 1, no. Committee of 9, yes. Committee of actions and deliverance. Committee of concern, appreciation and endeavors are as in every action of faith. Now to change the world is to first change the hearts of men. Goodness is a Godly nature and only the evils of man are more forceful due to the ways of mans' observance. So let us prepare to begin another new phase of growth, learning and development. This day, as council chairman do you sit. Thus goals set are by you.

As council chairman, again unto you, falls the duty of actions to portray an active attempt. . . .To accept aids thru us is to gain and maintain momentum in numerous directions. To qualify is unnecessary—only acceptance of position. Qualifying has long since been. Now, go. Prepare family, for day's learning and adventure are indeed the steps of necessity. After this gala event of visitations is joyfully climaxed will time be.

Adieu.

I did my housework, prepared for supper and the snacks after school then wanted some more answers. I had become accustomed to the writing and receiving answers to write down, but this seeing was a lot different! I asked only, "Can you give me a sample of what the new phase will be like?"

To be ready. To be eager. To be at peace with self due to confidence of actions. Jesus of Nazareth has, this day, granted all pleas. Forthcoming are the many rigors of and reaping of the many meaningful possessions of mankind toward which he sets his goals. Attached to trials fall responsibilities of labor and trusting in physical capabilities. But herein lies another way. One of following

Council of Angels

where our saviour led. One of giving to be given to and one of thankfulness to God and acknowledging His hand as that of the giver. To be as ever a symbol for all to see and wonder. To be as a beacon light on a high hill and to be ever a burning bright light—dimmed by none, to be sought. . .and sought after for guidance of a lasting nature. To turn a friendly cup of coffee into a cup of loving care, supped as by a thirsty man. Leave all doubts and go forward on all counts.

During the next few days I was busy with business. I made deliveries to several locations and visited with many customers and co-workers. I enthusiastically wrote for any one who told me they were bogged down with a problem. My housework was caught up and the food preparations for the coming week had been organized. I was feeling pretty proud of my self. I surely had everything done.

Friday May 28, 1976: 8: am. "Anything?

Progress made in many areas. Accomplishments of tasks at home, contacts of concerned peoples and furtherments in business. Let's set aside a time for correspondence and a time to write. Also concern yourself with publications of written materials. Investigate sources of query into realms unto now unfamiliar in church relations—reincarnation and Bible—and become an active novice. Supplant the interest of relying on, to relying in Christ. There is a difference. 'On' indicates outside. 'In' indicates part of and related to. Once part of and related to is to never become separated from. Absent, yes, but even absent is still the same part of and the same related to. Only in ways of deliberate action of severance can one become no longer a member, but only in actions not in reality—formulating games of intrigue.

"I thought I had things under control and now you bring up all of this. What do you mean by formulate games of intrigue?"

By trying new ways. Say: Let's, hereby release action of unseen powers. . .believed unavailable. Say: Let's get and keep this house in smooth running order. Say: Let's get this business in order; Let's set time to get to worship; And assemble committee to contact areas of unrest. Of course locations are beyond you. . .in your grasp lies devious ways of advancements in all areas.

"Devious ways? Are these bad ways?"

Not bad—a little different approach—one of more interest. Prayer is a different way for most. Prayers are maximum security. Prayers are the same measures as a vault. To become doubtful rusts the hinges and then the contents are forgotten. Prayers can become unanswered at mans' expected time, for many are the workings of labors of the unseen realm's activities. Thus does the prayer come to expect naught. These are stages. Learning and process of developments become feelings of security instead of feelings of need. A development which takes time and a process which comes of devious works from angelic hoards, but actions made by unseen forces change the feeling and desires of man to teach a surer and a more secure way of life on earth and cause mans' realization of much changing in the lives touched. Church? Go and pray often. Worship with others as opportunity offers. Rejoice.

"Assemble *my* Committee? What are you talking about?"

As it was the first time we met, to see did you position yourself in a comfortable position and expect answers to daily living. So, did we assemble. This to be a customary and acceptable way to start the day or even the week, but daily contact is by far the most desirous ways.

"O.K. I can do that. How do I know you'll be able to be there when I'm ready?"

We are ever available. Are the stars and moon not there in the heat of mid-day sun? No, only absent of sight due to brightness of day. Yet are they ever there. This also is our way. To become seen is of our jurisdiction according to the laws of the universal spirit. Can you force the sightings of the moon and stars in noon day sun? Nor can you force our visual countenance.

"I wonder why in the world I'm shown your countenance and what did I ever do to reach this place in life!"

For man to conceive and immediately perceive is too much to believe. Lay it aside. Only abide.

"O.K. Now, about the publishing of written materials. I'm sure you mean the little book. Here I thought it would be a book of five hundred pages or more and it is only a few. I don't know how I'm going to get it in print, but I will find a way. This week. I will be tuned to your guidance as to where to go. Also, the money needed to get it printed. Wonder where that will come from and how much it will take. All for now. I've much to do!"

Council of Angels

Familiar Ground

June 7, 1976.
"Any messages today?"
Purity, simplicity and faith are attributes of necessity. To first belie beliefs of fathers, forefathers and various teachers, who, over the space of time, delve not, but accept only that which has previously been recorded, are ways of few. Then to gently relay the findings for others to be introduced to is again an avenue of oneness of self and of adventure into new an untried fields. Delving into books of other's ideas and experiences and delving into experiences of your own curiosity are putting you onward. Finding first, then accepting, are two steps and the starting of each must first be preceded by actions and then follow-up actions. To have selected a committee is a gigantic step. To have accepted as a reality is again a gigantic step and now, to rely on their presence to actively deliver material in abundance is again to stride forward. So now. . .put problems of business into our midst and thus condone all actions of delivery unto our jurisdiction.

"Are you telling me I don't have to telephone Dallas? You had better come in mighty loud and clear on this one!"

I am telling you: Put on us the deliverance of all merchandise.

"How do I do this?"

Say: . . .to my committee do I trust all deliverance of merchandise, even including jewels of past orders. And also of this date do I commend all past and all future orders unto your jurisdiction to be updated no later than the 15th of this month; to keep current and correct all correspondence and literature of necessary development. This is action—not of mans' usual concept but of a much higher concept and. . .in use of faith, trust and (for men) simplicity.

"Well, you are right on that one. For man this is not simple and sure is a new way of doing things for me. However, I'm saying this to my committee. So, I'll wait till the 15th of this month and leave it in your care. Anything else for now?"

Let's, together, be of confidence in daily tasks and turn home into valuable shinning treasure house of charm, peace and living love.

In my direct-sales business the merchandise, which I paid for at the time of placing the order, was many months behind. I needed the merchandise to deliver to customers so they could pay me, replenishing my money.

"O.K. I will do my housework and enjoy doing it. I will not worry about the back shipments of merchandise."

I turned on the radio to a fast-paced music; opened the

Council of Angels

doors and windows and really was into my housework when the door bell rang. The United Parcel man was holding one large cardboard box and two were at his feet. Wow! I said to him, Looks like I finally got some orders!

As it turned out, I hadn't received any of the back orders of jewelry but I did receive all of my last three orders! This was a first for many months. As I unpacked and checked the products I was wondering how it was possible this order arrived after I had written this very morning. At 2:45 p.m.—the stuff was nearly here at the time I had written. I went back to find some answers.

"I received my $800.00 order complete. No back orders, but to not have any new back orders is a plus. Now, how is it that I wrote only this morning and received the shipment in a few hours? Are you in the recesses of my mind or how could I have known this? Is this coincidence? You have said there were no coincidences. Then how is this explained?"

Let us say. . .the mind processes awareness as you contact us. . .a medium little used by man. As a sub conscious—no. As an extra development of yourself to cause self to gyrate or do excessive physical traits—no. As a development thru your mind's capacity to contact and relay necessities and thus set to motion this realm of activity to fulfillment of your actual material needs—yes.

"My understanding is no clearer."

Many are the treasures life holds, many are the trusts

and many the pangs of learning. The circumstances of individuals differ for each individual's purpose of learning. Processing life's experiences are as a stewing in a preserve kettle. Actions reach a turmoil—boiling—but come out sweeter and more useful and last longer.

"I give up. Only will I accept what you send me as I need it."

Words of My Own

I searched the telephone books and newspapers for a printer. None of those I contacted printed books. Many other types of printing, but not books.

While driving through the city where I bought groceries I noticed a new printing shop. Immediately, I knew this was the one I had been looking for.

The man at the counter assured me they did print books.

I handed him my few sheets of typed paper and told him I would like them in a book form. After he measured and etc. he informed me, This will make a 16-page book. If the number of pages were less it would be called a pamphlet, but 16 is a book. If you want to get it copyrighted I can give you the form to fill out and the address where to send it.

I was delighted. Also, felt happy for this man. I knew he was a reformed alcoholic. This was his new start in life. I did not mention this to him and wondered why I knew the book was to be in print in twenty days. It cost me $200.00

for 1,000 books. I paid the man one hundred and the other hundred would be due when I picked the books up. I had the hundred dollars in my billfold from selling the merchandise I had received two days before and sold. It was no problem at all. I was really excited. This had been so easy! Getting my chores done in town, I seemed to be walking on air. I was so excited and thrilled. As soon as I arrived home I collected my pen and note book to write the latest update.

"This is so exciting! I have the little book at the printers and it will be done within twenty days.

"O.K. Now, for next problem. Our son-in-law is upset with his job. Needs another, yet this means a change of college and schools for his wife and child. Should she drop school and they move to a new job?"

For what benefit? Surely assuming a debt and dropping a task is of no benefit. But in fact—of great hindrance. He will adjust in a little while. Slight discomforts are as a pair of too tight shoes. They pass the point of endurance.

"Well, then, he can't stand this much longer. Will you show him a better move than the one he plans? Can you do it?"

He can be free. Til then must he be of great patience.

Put one room in order and start to play—not the role of tired ol' woman; but one of gaiety, assurance, and rested— one of blessings, endurance and withstanding all testings. A new way of life and to all a blessing.

"I feel I've not yet accomplished your commands of organizing my duties."

Council of Angels

Before all this great knowledge. . .you did not question so and the way was made. So now can also be made a way. Repaying debts of year's collections will become apparent with knowledge. Friendships extended are as fences mended—always are repairs needed and appreciated. Sharing is as repairing another's fences. Many are the attempts but sincerity of need is the cause of deed. Read 'Romans 4 and 5'.

Four days later a call from our daughter saying her husband's conditions at his work had leveled off and he was not having the difficulties he had been experiencing. He had decided to not take the position in a distant state. I was grateful. I wrote: "Words are inadequate—but my appreciation of your presence is sweet. Our precious family are on a more secure condition. How do I say thanks? Don't know how you did this, just glad."

To know details of events are not the ways of man. All enticements, expectations and mysteries of events to come would dim the varnish as water moisture from a damp towel. When God's blessings unfold they are as radiant beams falling on an unpolluted stream. A glory for all to behold and then will the recounting of events be told and listened to and held in great awe. Peace, now, and gratefulness of the present gifts of painlessness, acquirements and trust. Cling, ever, to these and hear in your heart songs of praise.

Upon completing the last sentence, I was aware of others in the room with me.

Jo Long

"Are all of my committee here?"
We are, as of this moment.
"I believe I have come a long way in my attitude about people, but I still become so disgusted and have a dirty mouth. Why is this?"
Developments of morals are a higher quality. . .The last to adapt is the mouth. Quickness of a tongue defiles air surrounding all individuals. To desire this improvement is a step in the right direction. Limitations on frustrations are fraught less until mouth control is under your jurisdiction. Remember what the mouth spews forth is from the depth of the spring. Does it boil up scum and sediment or only goodness of sweet water? Also—to what avail? Leave us to handle our task as preset and rest yourself, then come to us with skirts cleaned and starched.
"O.K.—I'm not going to question why I'm so lucky to have you. I'm only glad I can accept you. I will still refer to you as spirits for I know of no other way. Surely somewhere is a reference I can turn to, one I and others can accept."
'Hebrews: 1:7, 1:14, 2:2, 2:4,' 'Colossians 1:16,' as a beginning.
Then, there is Job, Psalms, Jude and Daniel.
"All of those passages? Why haven't you shown me before?"
Acceptance of a timely nature.
As I read the verses I was amazed.
'Hebrews: 1:7': God speaks of his angels as messengers swift as the wind and as servants made of flaming fire.

Council of Angels

'Hebrews 1:14': for the angels are only spirit-messengers sent out to help and care for those who are to receive his salvation. '2:2': for since the messages from angels have always proved true.
How about that. We talk with angels!

After this I studied for a long time searching passages and wondered why I could not have found them before. They seemed to literally jump off the page. The Bible was actually coming to life for me. I had to find out what else was in it!

I have learned that God's angels are active. They are busy helping people. On earth. Today. They are waiting to be asked. They are available to all—only if they are asked.

Remember, "angels can only sit on a rock and wait until they are asked for." Then do they become active for the individual who sought them and actually asked God to send help. The way to do that is simply say, "Hey, God, I need you. Show me the way."

Then give yourself a chance to be led to goodness by setting aside a time for quietness. Make a commitment of a special time to put all worldly things aside and listen—don't be impatient, but listen—as for the flutter of a butterfly wing, for the things of God to be revealed to you.

Each person has their own experiences. Perhaps as a startling, instantaneous revelation, or in a slower more gentle way over a period of time. Extra stress and pressure of a three-day span can be expected as a testing stage where one needs to be determined to stick to their commitment. Doubt can consume you, but don't let it. Remember, not only do you have a Guardian Angel—you have a committee of angels at your beck and call. They are waiting to be of help to you, whatever your needs. I believe they are the highest and best sources of aid to mankind sent through Jesus Christ from God.

Although my life's story continues, on this note I will close this book of experiences. It is my wish for each reader to find the peace of mind and the mysteries of the universal creation to benefit their walk on earth. Peace.

Council of Angels

The author with her husband, Charles "Huey" Long, also a writer, best known for his humorous short stories represented in his book, *Coon Tales & Cockle Burs.*

Watch for other
Interesting Books for Interesting People
by
Mayhaven Publishing
P O Box 557
Mahomet, IL 61853

Also watch for books from our other imprint:
Wild Rose Publishing

Books, the perfect gift for any occasion.